A Clarified Vision
for Urban Mission

Books by Harvie M. Conn

Contemporary World Theology

Theological Perspectives on Church Growth (editor)

Evangelism: Doing Justice and Preaching Grace

Eternal Word and Changing Worlds

Reaching the Unreached (editor)

Missions and Theological Education in World Perspective
       (co-editor)

A Clarified Vision for Urban Mission

A Clarified Vision for Urban Mission

Dispelling the Urban Stereotypes

Harvie M. Conn

Zondervan Publishing House • Grand Rapids, MI

A CLARIFIED VISION FOR URBAN MISSION
Copyright © 1987 by Harvie M. Conn

MINISTRY RESOURCES LIBRARY is an imprint of Zondervan Publishing House,
1415 Lake Drive, S.E., Grand Rapids, Michigan 49506.

Library of Congress Cataloging in Publication Data

Conn, Harvie M.
    A clarified vision for urban mission.

    Bibliography: p.
    Includes indexes.
    1. Cities and towns—Religious aspects—Christianity. 2. Sociology, Urban.
3. City churches. 4. City missions. I. Title.
BR115.C45C66   1987   253'.09173'2   86-23611
ISBN 0-310-45441-7

Edited by James E. Ruark
Designed by Louise Bauer

Printed in the United States of America

87 88 89 90 91 92 / EP / 10 9 8 7 6 5 4 3 2 1

To the administration and students of the
Center for Urban Theological Studies

Contents

Preface

In every culture the stereotypes and myths about the city abound. A 1965 study of present-day Iraq traces all the best of the Iraqi city dweller—physical courage, loyalty among kinsmen, generosity, honesty, hospitality—to the pastoral ancestor. Any weakening of these virtues is due to the deteriorating influence of the city.[1] Urban life in the Middle East becomes civilized but degenerate, nomadic culture savage but noble.

Religious beliefs dying in the city is still another stereotype. A middle-aged woman repeats it to me after a worship service in a suburban white church: "You're closer to God in the country." Yet the 1984 annual Gallup poll on religion in America sees no large gap between center city, suburb, or rural area on a question like "How important is religion in your own life?" Fifty-three percent of those who live in the center city answer "very important." In the suburbs 51 percent feel that way, in the rural areas 61 percent.[2] A difference to be sure, but not large enough to carry the weight of the stereotype.

The list continues: too much crime in the city, too many poor, too many people. And flowing from these generalizations come the fears. The labels read anonymity, depersonalization, marginalization, secularization. They paralyze Christian initiative to reach cities for Christ, they are stumbling blocks in the way of urban church planting, they send Christian leaven and salt running for safety on suburban kitchen shelves.

This book is an effort at evangelical demythologizing about the city. It looks for grains of truth in the generalizations and tries to shovel away the accumulated snowdrifts. It is not a book about Christian strategy for urban evangelization. We still have too little information to write such a "how-to-do-it" manual. And cities are too different for just one such manual. Our aim is more modest: a preliminary look at urban realities, cutting away the mythical underbrush and weeds.

To do the job we make use of three tools especially—the insights of urban sociology, urban anthropology, and biblical theology. It is a small exercise in the trialogue we have pled for in an earlier book, a case study in contextualization.[3] Linking all these tools together is our missionary intention, calling our cities to Christ.

Some of the materials have already appeared in print. I am grateful to the editors of *Reformed Review, Evangelical Journal,* and *Urban Mission* for permission to incorporate parts of essays originally appearing in their journals in expanded or contracted form in this book. Significant parts of chapters 1–2, 4–5 are drawn from earlier publications in these periodicals.

I am especially grateful to Roger and Edna Greenway, colleagues in the study and teaching of urban missions at Westminster Theological Seminary, for their encouragement and stimulation in thinking through many of the ideas that now appear in hard print. William Krispin, the director of the Center for Urban Theological Studies, has been, all along the way, a fellow dreamer about the city of God. My indebtedness to the staff and students at the Center is incalculable. Dave Garnett, Trudy Collins, Wilbert Richardson, Adele Brooks, Wesley Pinnock, so many others—they are all my teachers in urban missions. They are representatives of the only church movement in North America that has embraced the city as God's mission field. The storefronts of the black church arose to meet a new need, not to flee from it. In prisons and on street corners, in ghettos and suburbs, they carry the word of the Lord. I am thankful to have a very small part in their mission to the city. This book is a partial payment of my debt to my brothers and sisters.

NOTES

[1] Ira M. Lapidus, ed., *Middle Eastern Cities* (Berkeley: University of California Press, 1969), p. 143.

[2] *Religion in America: The Gallup Report. Report No. 222* (Princeton: Princeton Religion Research Center, 1984), p. 34.

[3] Harvie M. Conn, *Eternal Word and Changing Worlds: Theology, Anthropology and Mission in Trialogue* (Grand Rapids: Zondervan, 1984).

The Rural/Urban Myth:
"It's the City,
What Do You Expect?"

Chapter One

The Rural/Urban Myth: "It's the City, What Do You Expect?"

The world is becoming more and more urban. At the beginning of this century, 15 percent of our world lived in cities. By 1950, that figure had risen to 28 percent. By 1975, it was 41 percent. By 2000, if the Lord tarries, it will reach at least 55 percent. At that time, at least 3.2 billion people will be living in cities, a total equal to the entire world's population in 1965.

Much of that growth is taking place in areas traditionally called mission fields. By the end of the century, more than two-thirds of the world's total urban population will be living in what are called less-developed countries. There the rate of urbanization is occurring three or four times as fast as the rate in industrialized countries. Mexico City will have thirty million by the end of this century. In each year of the mid-1970s, São Paulo grew by more than a quarter-million people. Jakarta and Seoul grew by more than a half-million people. Within two decades, the urban population of the Third World countries will be close to 41 percent. It was less then 16 percent in 1950.[1] The world spawns virtually a new Chicago every month or so.

Latin America has become the most highly urbanized region in the developing world. Currently 61 percent of the Latin American population lives in cities of 20,000 or more, an increase of 22 percent since 1950. Between 1960 and 1970, the hemisphere's total population increased approximately 2.8 percent annually. But its rural regions grew by only 1.3 percent annually. Six countries—Argentina, Brazil, Chile, Mexico, Peru, and Venezuela—comprise 73 percent of the total; these six countries contain 639 of the approximately 800 cities of 20,000 or more people in the region. Every year between 1985 and 2000, more than 11 million new persons will live in Latin American cities. The urbanization process took more than a century in the United States and Canada; in Latin America it is being compressed into a few short decades.

Africa is the least urbanized of the continents. In 1980, only one out of four people in Africa lived in urban areas. Yet Peter Gutkind says that "it has the fastest rate of urban growth in the world."[2] The United Nations estimates that between 1850 and 1950, Africa's annual rate of urban growth was at least 3.9 percent compared with 2.6 percent for the world as a whole. The rise of the cities is one of the most significant events behind the great transformation of contemporary Africa. North Africa is the most urbanized. All the countries bordering the Mediterranean Sea have between two-fifths and three-fifths of their population in places of 20,000 or more inhabitants.

Generalizations about Asia are difficult to make. Until two hundred years ago, Asia contained more city dwellers than the rest of the world combined. If present demographic trends continue, by the year 2000 Asia again will have more city dwellers than any other continent. At least one-third of the total urban population of the world will be in Asia.

Statistics for the Anglo-Saxon world are equally startling. Figures for 1972 based on population living in cities of 100,000 or more list Australia as 84.4 percent urban, North America 75.1 percent, and Europe 63 percent.

Sadly, however, city evangelism and church planting have not been on the agenda of the church. "After a hundred and fifty years of modern missions, the plain fact is that churches have not done well in most cities of Africasia."[3] Some of this is simply due to strategy demands. As late as 1900, six-sevenths of the world's population was rural. Mission boards were structured to meet those rural needs. The history of missions is dotted with names like China Inland Mission, Africa Inland Mission, Sudan Interior Mission. All bear testimony to the call of the rural when that call was urgent. That was wise strategy then, and it still is in some places.

But now half the human race lives in cities, with some urban centers like Bogotá growing at a rate of 4,000 to 6,000 persons per day. New commitments are required. Meeting them, however, remains difficult. North America continues to send the vast majority of missionaries into the world. But few of these candidates for the mission field view the Scriptures or the world through urban eyes. A book by James D. Hunter in 1983 notes that "evangelicals are grossly underrepresented in the large cities." Only 8.6 percent surveyed by Hunter were in cities of one million or more.[4]

How can we recruit personnel for reaching our urban generations when the rural and suburban areas have nurtured their visions of the church? Why is the North American mission movement still deeply oriented to tribal, rural, or suburban settings? Why, in our borrowed church-growth definitions of the unfinished task, do we still speak of groupings in terms of common cultures of origin—Hindus, Muslims, Chinese?

Urban scientists increasingly question the wisdom of restricting our definitions of urbanization largely by ethnic standards. Urban groupings are more and more defined in terms of macrostructural social classes, the social groups structured around wealth, power, and prestige. Or to smaller social units who create community and neighborhood around occupations or lifestyle interests. In the preindustrial city, occupation, ethnicity, and neighborhood tend to be overlapping membership units; they share common boundaries. But in the industrial city or the city in developing nations, these three units show less overlap; they rarely share common boundaries.[5] By contrast, this sophisticated level of discussion is missing in evangelical church planning. Thinking remains dominated by ethnicity. Planting an urban church frequently is defined today as planting an ethnic church.

Why is this? What are the barriers that hinder wider strategy planning?

THE RURAL/URBAN MYTHOLOGY

A major factor to my mind is the contemporary rural mythology that lies behind so much of our academic thinking and theorizing in the industrial age. Drawing on the paradigm of "the noble savage," verbalized by Jean Jacques Rousseau, the myth romanticizes the bucolic countryside and gazes in horror at the city. Its deep-level character may help to explain the faddish, short-lived response given to Harvey Cox's *Secular City* and his ill-fated effort to sacralize urban secularity. Theories do not stand up well against deep-set mythologies.

In its present state, this is a fairly recent twist to the myth. The city was not viewed so negatively in other times and places as it is in present-day, industrial societies. During the Middle Ages, Western cities were associated with choice and freedom; serfs who escaped to the city and could remain there for a certain period were legally freed. Early medieval monasticism was a movement against the cities; monasteries were established in solitary and remote areas away from the population centers. But by the time the mendicant orders arose in the thirteenth century, this anti-urban, pro-rural bias had shifted. The Jesuits earned the title of "megalopolitans"; the Franciscans and Dominicans began to build in the early Gothic cities.[6] During the Enlightenment, cities again became centers of culture and knowledge.

The formation of the English language reflected this flattering but temporary picture of the city. Wilfred Funk notes,

We citydwellers, at least in ancient days, were supposed to be more *civil* in our manners and more *civilized* in our ways than others, for both of these words, *civil* and *civilized,* are the eventual children of the Latin term *civis* which meant "one who lives in the city." All city folks, you see, were regarded as automatically cultured and well housebroken. And from the ancient Latin we have borrowed the word *urbs* which also meant city, and we used it to create the word *urbane* which describes the smooth manners that were presumed to be characteristic of *metropolitan* society. . . . And from the Greek *polis,* "city," we inherited our word *politic.* If you are *politic,* you are expedient, shrewd, discreet, and artful in your address and your procedure which sounds dangerously like a city slicker![7]

With the eighteenth century, this anti-rural attitude reversed. During the industrial revolution there was a coalescence of industrialization and urban growth. And out of it came a renewal of the polarized mythology, this time on the rural side. There was a renewed fear of urban life as dehumanizing. The city became a symbol of social disorder and artificiality, anomie and chaos. And that picture was mythic in proportion. It permeates the popular as well as the academic view of city life.

What this means is explained in *Anthropology of the City* by Edwin Eames and Judith G. Goode:

Thus when a news magazine, radio, or television news department produces an urban affairs segment, this usually means the reporting of crime, poverty, low-income housing and assorted miseries. The view of the city as unnatural can be demonstrated by a recent TV advertisement for Boy Scouting depicting a forlorn boy wandering through the city. The message states that this boy lives in a shoddy, non-genuine world: "His stars are neon lights. Instead of grass, he has cement." Boys are urged to join the Boy Scouts and engage in camping to spend time in the countryside, get away from the urban scene. Thus they will become more human.[8]

In 1974 the *Philadelphia Inquirer* published a study ranking American cities on the basis of "quality of life" indexes. It was titled "There Are No Good U.S. Cities, Only Less Bad."[9] When the author discussed city features he assumed everyone would favor, the first to be mentioned was plentiful parklands. As critics of that article have pointed out, many of the "good" criteria of the cities cited are basically non-urban. Another measure of "goodness" was lower density of population. Presumably a higher density of trees is more important to urban children than a high density of playmates. In the article, the best city becomes the least citylike.

This anti-urban mentality is more than a bias. It is a mythology and continues to remain so in the church. Truman B. Douglass can thus speak of "The Job Protestants Shirk" and comment, "There are three great areas of our world which churches have not really penetrated. They are: Hinduism, Islam and the culture of our modern cities."[10] A missions executive at a meeting of the Evangelical Foreign Missions Association in 1983 can say to the author, "God made the country and man made the suburb. But the devil made the city." He could laugh when he said it. I cannot.

FROM MYTHOLOGY TO SCIENCE

The beginnings of sociology and cultural anthropology coincided with the mythical turn against the city and found ways to reinforce it. Ferdinand Tönnies (1855–1936) transformed the polarization into two contrasting types of human social life, *Gemeinschaft* and *Gesellschaft*. *Gemeinschaft* is community, the lifestyle of the small country village. Here people work for the common good, linked by ties of family and neighborhood, common interests and purposes. Its lifestyle is one of "intimate, private and exclusive living together," a sense of "Our-ness." *Gesellschaft,* by contrast, is merely association, the mechanical life of the city. In such a mentality, natural ties of kinship, neighborhood, and friendship tend to decline. Life becomes more rational, more calculating.

The European school followed Tönnies in his "theory of

contrasts." But not all were as negative as he. Emile Durkheim (1858–1917) turned against the rural. Its "solidarity" was "mechanical." The city and its "organic solidarity" offered for Durkheim greater hope and freedom for society. Out of the city, he affirmed, would come a new form of social cohesion based on mutuality and interdependence.

Europeans had set the agenda. American sociologists, associated with what came to be called the Chicago school, not only adopted the contrast theory but reinforced Tönnies's negative conclusions about life in the city. Under the leadership of Robert Park (1864–1944), Louis Wirth (1897–1952), and Ernest Burgess, the myth acquired scientific status.

Both Park and Wirth saw the possibility of greater freedom in the city. But they saw also that the city was an acid that, in time, would eat away traditional values and undermine the formation of meaningful institutions and relationships. Wirth especially worried that any positive aspects would be compromised by disorganization and alienation bred in the city environment. Park and Wirth's fears were reinforced by the on-site studies they promoted. Their concern for urban disorganization, coupled with the need to focus research on more narrowed bands of the urban population, produced works on the hobo, the slum, the juvenile delinquent, the taxi hall dancer, the professional thief.[11]

The legacy of urban sociology passed to urban anthropology through the work of Robert Redfield, the son-in-law of Park and virtually the founder of the new discipline. His 1930 study, *Tepoztlan: A Mexican Village,* eulogized the peasant and folk community and was deeply influenced by the neo-Romantic view of rural life embodied in the sociological polarization of the rural and the urban structured by Tönnies. Assuming a unilinear evolution of culture from the simple to the complex, Redfield sought to study in his field work the progressive development of society from the tribe to the village to the city. His typology became the background for the attention of anthropology in the 1950s to "peasant societies." And behind much of it was the pastoral idea of Tepoztlan and the folk culture of the Yucatan as the idyllic model.

Anthropologists remained by no means happy with Redfield's conclusions. Gideon Sjoberg's 1960 work, *The Preindustrial City,* questioned the propriety of Redfield's implicitly accepting industrial cities as a universal urban model. Preindustrial cities, he argued, do not share the characteristics of impersonality, secularism, and great size assumed in the folk–urban contrast. In 1951, Oscar Lewis published *Life in a Mexican Village: Tepoztlan Restudied,* in which he found major faults with Redfield's model.[12] By 1954, Redfield, with M. B. Singer, was prepared to offer a large number of self-corrections to his earlier model.[13] Recent studies depend less and less on relations and tensions between city and rural populations, folk and urban.

FROM THE BEHAVIORAL SCIENCES TO THEOLOGY

Theology has never existed in isolation from the models of the behavioral sciences. The developmentalist models of E. B. Tylor and Sir James Frazer in the nineteenth century were drawn from the same paradigms that Julius Wellhausen made use of in his reconstruction of Israel's religious history. The diffusionist arguments of Wilhelm Schmidt crossed the academic line and created the Pan-Babylonian school. The History of Religions school used a neo-diffusionist paradigm in their search for the origins of Pauline theology in the mystery religions.[14]

In particular, the rural-urban polarization pattern has been prominent in contemporary Old Testament studies. And, as usual, such patterns in theological studies retain a longer lifespan than their behavioral science counterparts. Outdated patterns are applied that no longer represent a consensus outside the theological area of study.

The bridge that linked the two disciplined areas was supplied by Max Weber (1864–1920). Looking for a case history to support his thesis regarding the parallel development of Protestantism and capitalism, Weber found it in what he took to be the socioeconomic development of Israel's religious history. That history, he argued, emerged out of the clash between Israel's early nomadic lifestyle and social system and the urban social organization imitated from the Canaanites. Premonarchic Israel was a society formed around a loose confederation of the tribes functioning with a "charismatic" type of leadership. The only tie that linked family, tribe, and clan was their covenant consciousness, their sense of being united in the worship of the same God. The later protest of the prophets about social conditions in Israel was against the loss of this nomadic ideal in favor of the Canaanite model of society, the concentration of power in the landowning aristocracy.[15]

Weber's thesis was quickly followed by the endorsements of Adolphe Lods and Antonin Causse. Lods's 1930 history of Israel emphasized the part of the prophets in their attempt to restore "the nomadic ideal" in preference to the urban society of Canaan. The prophets became the spokesmen for an ideal of simplicity derived from the tradition of the desert, still alive in the lower classes.

Modifications of this sociological approach to the Old Testament came from American scholars like Louis Wallis and William C. Graham. Wallis sought to trace the ethical monotheism of the eighth-century prophets to a clash between urbanized Canaanite society and the more austere morality of the rural, wilderness cultural patterns of the Hebrews. Graham joined Wallis in seeing monotheism as the end-result of a slow process of growth. But he saw it less as a "return to the nomadic past" and more as "a process of regeneration" of the disintegrating culture pattern.

Some more influential support of the nomadic-urban tension came from the form-critical studies of Albrecht Alt and Martin Noth and their research of the social organization of the early settlement period. Alt, for example, elevated the nomadic to an ideal and characterized the earliest level of piety in the Hebrew Bible to the tribes still living outside the sphere of ancient urban civilization. The ancient Hebrews were seen as believing in gods not connected with permanent shrines or cities. Their religion was clearly a-city, if not anti-city. The assumptions characteristic of the rural-urban polarization controlled Alt's picture of non-urban Hebrew theology: (1) every human society was seen as evolving through a fixed series of lifestyles, that is, from hunter to nomad to sedentary villager to city dweller, and (2) hostility between nomadic and sedentary groups was seen as inevitable.[16]

From Weber's original work came other borrowings. Alt and Noth used the idea of clan-groups bound into a loose confederation or amphictyony through the covenant ideal. Israel's laws were said to reflect the nomadic ideal which assumed that the people stood against its urban environment instead of being part of it. Municipal traditions within the Mosaic corpus, such as case laws, were not authentically Israelite; they were seen to be adapted to the Jahwist faith.

Theories behind the nomadic ideal continue to be modified. William Foxwell Albright, for example, along with Cyrus Gordon, has insisted that not all Israel's ancestors were nomads. Abraham is regarded as the governor of an urban league. Studies in the covenant formulary, opened up by George Mendenhall, have drawn attention to Hittite parallels. And that Hittite empire was an urban culture, making the covenant genre an urban instrument. More recently Denis Baly has examined "the geography of monotheism" and pointed out, in contrast to nineteenth-century scholarship, that most city dwellers and nomads are polytheists. This prompted a critic to say, "Monotheism, according to Baly, has never developed in desert cultures; monotheism always develops in cities!"[17] Even law throughout the Ancient Near East, it is now argued, is an instrument by which cities protect and govern their citizens.

At the same time, the polarization seems to remain. Even as Albright offers his correctives to earlier theory, he also sees the conflict between Israel and the city as a duel to the death. So for Albright, the settlement history reflected in the Book of Joshua is the history of Israel sweeping across Canaan like a fury, leaving the cities smoldering in her wake. Albright's invasion theory, though in contrast to earlier immigration theories, is still built out of the dichotomy. The prophets become anti-urbanists. To the writer of Amos the cities become places where the poor are oppressed, commerce supplanting community, the old life of the desert people giving way to the settled life, and its temptations yielding to urban idolatry.

Among contemporary Bible interpreters, one stands out on the subject of the city. It has been said that "none has pursued this negative view of the city as one theme of the Bible with more drastic consistency than Jacques Ellul."[18] In Ellul's book *The Meaning of the City* (1970), the city becomes the place of idolatry, oppression, and opposition of human power to the power of God. The very fact of living in the city drives humanity down an inhuman road. The prophets and the Book of Revelation present the city as the place on earth where the conflict between God and humanity is carried to its highest pitch, where all the powers in revolt gather together. Only the resurrection of Jesus, a divine miracle of grace, can drastically reduce this pretension.[19]

Perhaps the fullest response yet to this anti-urban mentality is offered in the 1983 book by Don C. Benjamin, *Deuteronomy and City Life*. Benjamin precedes a full analysis of the city text in Deuteronomy with a careful summary of the cumulative arguments against the nomadic ideal. He interacts also with anthropological studies, making good use of the questions raised by Gideon Sjoberg in this same connection. His conclusion is that the city texts under examination betray a clear "urban tradition . . . which goes all the way back to Jahwists who lived together in cities during the 13th century BCE." And since this is so, "Biblical histories and theologies can no longer consider early Israel to be completely non-urban!"[20]

Similar corrections are offered by Frank Frick in *The City in Ancient Israel* (1977). Concentrating more on the monarchy period and the prophetic word concerning the city, Frick makes even more extensive use of Sjoberg's study of the preindustrial city. He discards earlier theory that overrated the particular socio-religious forms of the city. The city, he concludes, had no such final value in itself. It is only "as a symbol of man's attempt to provide for his own material security" that it stands condemned by the prophetic word.[21]

Whether Benjamin and Frick will finally steer biblical scholarship away from some longstanding assumptions remains to be seen. The old ways die hard.[22]

EVANGELICAL THINKING AND THE CITY

Does the evangelical escape this anti-urban bias? With Dwight L. Moody, they confess responsibility for the city's salvation: "If we can stir them, we shall stir the whole nation."[23] But, like Moody also, our calls for city revival reach mainly middle-class churchgoers. Moody's response to this reception was a retreat from the largest cities after the 1870s, first by confining himself to the smaller interior cities and then by gradually withdrawing from evangelistic work to concentrate on the Bible schools he had founded in Chicago and Northfield, Massachusetts.

> "We cannot get the people we are after," he lamented, when urged to resume urban revivalism. "The city is no place for me," he wrote his family in 1896 on a rare visit to New York. "If it was not for the work I am called to do, I would never show my head in this city or any other again."[24]

Contemporary evangelicals show a similar reluctance in urban mission strategy. They respond positively to the writings of Francis Schaeffer, who uses the image of the city as an affirmation "that we live in a post-Christian world." Schaeffer cries, "There is death in the *polis*. *There is death in the city*."[25] And the evangelical says Amen. Why?

Is the basic problem the failure of evangelicals to see the mythological character of their picture of the city? A myth is not a scientific creation, though it may be supported by the facts unearthed by science. It is rather a creation of the human heart designed to explain our cosmos and its relationship to God and our fellow human beings. It is intended as a rhetorical question asking, who are we, who is God, what is our world? And, like all rhetorical questions, it assumes itself to be irrefutable. Proverbs become its logical method.

Like all mythology spun by the images of God, it carries within itself the contradictions of its society, knit together in a fragile effort to conceal the polarizations it wants to avoid.[26] Sometimes one element of that polarity becomes apparent, sometimes another. History's pendulum swing sometimes discloses one, sometimes another.

So in the United States, the urban myth is inextricably linked with her civil religion, the American Dream, the "good society" where the "happiest state of man is the middle state between the savage and the refined, or between the wild and the luxurious state."[27] The myth incorporates into the Dream the agrarian bias toward simplicity, farming, virtue, and republicanism associated with Thomas Jefferson. And alongside it is the vision of America captured in the 1840 painting by Thomas Cole, "The Architect's Dream." One-half of the canvas reveals a city of dazzling classical architecture, the other half a dark forest with a Gothic church. Out of the "wilderness" comes the fruitful city.

Thus it is that the church's vision and America's picture of the city fluctuate between these contrary images. Like Walt Whitman, we seem to think of ourselves as the poets of the city and as the poets of nature. We yearn to have "both worlds." In the late nineteenth and early twentieth centuries, the myth turns to the dark side of the pole, the beauty of the vision scarred by the horror of industrialization and the brutal side of capitalism. The Pilgrim's Progress model drives the white, middle-class creator of the mythology to the suburbs, where the decaying of the Dream may be preserved in the moral homogeneity of a new kind of village. In the Exodus retreat, the church follows from the 1950s, still looking for an insulated, social consensus of nice people, black following white in captivity to the same American Hope. The Dream is portable and still affordable. "At least we still have the suburbs," consoled one church executive. "This is basically a suburban society, and we have our strength in the suburbs."[28]

DEMYTHOLOGIZING THE CITY

How will we demolish this myth? Until it crumbles, we will continue to retreat not only from the cities of the United States, but from the cities of the world. World mission will continue to be reduced to suburban mission. Yet several factors are reinforcing our resistance to demythologizing.

1. Our cultural reading of the Bible is one of the roadblocks. It was an open Bible in the life of the city that unleashed an urban Reformation in the sixteenth century. Calvin's socioeconomic impact on Geneva earned him the title "the Constructive Revolutionary."[29] And by the end of that century, fifty of the sixty-five imperial cities subject to the emperor officially recognized the sovereign call of God to Europe's Ninevehs. John Piet reminds us of the symbol of that ministry in a mural which graces the Missionary Center of the Reformed Churches at Baarn, the Netherlands.

> It shows an elderly Calvin standing behind a young, modern missionary. Even though four hundred years lie between them, the two are one, because the hand of Calvin points over the young man's shoulder to the open Bible he holds in his hand.[30]

But the history we sketched earlier in this chapter reminds us that too often mythological two-by-fours in our own eye escape the attention while we look for slivers in·the eyes of others (Matt. 7:3). American Dreams can cloud our visions of the city; unexamined models created by our cultural world views affect the facts we choose to see or not see in the Scriptures. Our theologies of the city must be constructed with one eye on the Bible and one eye on the place where we put up our church signs. John Piet put it correctly: "Accordingly, with the hand of the Reformers upon us, let us turn to the Bible and examine the church in the context of the world today."

2. Another roadblock is that *the American Dream is a middle-class dream.* Gibson Winter writes that historically the identification of Christianity with the middle and upper classes in Western Europe

> seems to be the primary factor in the decline of Christian churches in Sweden, England and France. Christianity has deep roots in these countries, but urbanization has undermined it for centuries. Urban Christianity in Western Europe has been concentrated among the bourgeoisie and has been alienated from the working classes.[31]

The picture is the same in North Africa. There Christianity identified with the upper social classes and disappeared without a trace as Islam swept across the southern Mediterranean.

We are not advocating here a return to the 1970s and what someone has called "the era of Wasp-swatting." Nor is the answer a biblical endorsement of world urban gentrification. We are calling for a renewed look at middle-class ideals and values and a warning at confusing them with the tenets of Christianity. The baptism of materialism in the name of Jesus, the benediction of competition as a way of life, the sanctification of growth as numerical success—all these hinder us from finding the invisible, urban poor and relating evangelism to "the underside of history," the urban world of the weak, the defeated, the "nonperson." The church, created in this image, becomes merely a warm spot for troubled souls.

Calvin's urban vision for Geneva was oriented to the underside. Christian concern for the poor, the sick, the orphan, the widow, the refugee was institutionalized in the diaconate and legislated by law. "Sumptuary laws" enacted in 1558 attacked "conspicuous consumption" and were actually a part of the war on poverty. A network of hospitals for the city, along with the requirement that each doctor visit the poor sick in the quarter in which he lived, came close to what some scholars today willingly label "socialized medicine."[32]

Calvin's example reads like an experiment in "the simple lifestyle," a call to kingdom moderation, to a holistic gospel.

3. Still another roadblock is *the privatization of our faith*. Our definition of making disciples stops short too frequently at the boundaries of personal and domestic life. Carl S. Dudley writes,

> The importance of the individual believer is at the center of the Christian affirmations of the American Dream. The individual believer expects fulfillment through personal faith, individual responsibility, and continued growth "in the nurture and admonition of the Lord." Individual response is the target of the Protestant invitation of faith. Individual responsibility is the basis for private morality. Individual growth is the assumption that motivates the believers to higher, more specialized levels of education and professional training.[33]

Our social conscience is limited frequently, then, to issues revolving around abortion, pornography, prayer in schools, and an occasional spot-check reference to euthanasia. Our theological definitions of salvation are more *ordo salutis* than *historia salutis*. This is reinforced by current fears we will be drawn into an ideology of the left and forced into searching for "kingdom signs" in political or economic liberation movements.

I sense the evangelical center moving with more freedom through some of these questions today. A consultation held in Grand Rapids, Michigan, in 1982, sponsored by the Lausanne Committee for World Evangelization and the World Evangelical Fellowship, is forcing us to think more carefully about the relationship of evangelism and social responsibility. Wheaton '83 and the International Conference on the Nature and Mission of the Church has reinforced a new and growing consensus that is growing around the idea of the kingdom of God. But the consensus is still a fragile and tender one. Many within the evangelical camp move further to the right. The Evangelical Statement issued at the Vancouver gathering of the World Council of Churches in 1983 will draw some further into the center but will push others to the edges, both right and left.

A more holistic perspective may be coming, if it is not crushed by a sharp swing in either direction. If that holism arrives, we may find a new openness toward the city. One cannot minister in the city, for the city, with only a vest-pocket Bible and a prayer list scratched on the back of a preacher's business card.

4. Racism remains behind much of what I have described, coloring our vision of the middle-class Dream. James D. Hunter writes, "Contemporary Evangelicalism is, of course, a white religious phenomenon."[34] Recent demographic studies indicate with surprise that

> the percentage of Evangelical blacks is lower than might be expected. Black religion has always been thought of as a "religion of the disinherited"—oriented toward salvation, revival, holiness, and biblical literalism—in a word, crudely Evangelical. Yet current data do not support this idea.[35]

The most visible display of this racism in recent years has been suburbanization and the evangelical church's retreat from the American cities in "white flight." A black brother said to me recently, "Integration is a white term to cover the period of time between the moving in of the first black and the moving out of the last white."

In the same spirit, whites will speak of "the church having abandoned the cities." The racism is still there, with whites defining "the church" as "our church," not "theirs."

A less visible demonstration of racism is evident in evangelical foreign missions activity. There are few if any minority people speaking for the world's cities on our mission boards. Those boards are almost totally monocultural. Where are the black mission executives in the Evangelical Foreign Missions Association (EFMA), the Interdenominational Foreign Missions Association (IFMA), and the Division of Missions, National Council of Churches of Christ in the U.S.A. (DOM)? Where are the Hispanics and the Asians who constitute more and more a rich part of North America's evangelical force? Why are there so few minority foreign missionaries when the history of the black in nineteenth-century foreign missions is such a rich one?[36] How can we plead for the evangelization of the cities of the world when those cities' major stockholders are not represented in our midst?

Space will not allow us to add to our list. Perhaps these alone are enough to work on in the coming chapters. Will the myth keep destroying us? Or will we have begun to destroy the myth?

NOTES

[1] Roger S. Greenway, ed., *Discipling the City* (Grand Rapids: Baker, 1979), p. 88.

[2] Peter Gutkind, *Urban Anthropology* (Assen, The Netherlands: Van Gorcum, 1974), p. 9.

[3] Donald A. McGavran, *Understanding Church Growth* (Grand Rapids: Wm. B. Eerdmans, rev. ed. 1980), p. 316.

[4] James D. Hunter, *American Evangelicalism: Conservative Religion and the Quandary of Modernity* (New Brunswick, N.J.: Rutgers University Press, 1983), pp. 52–53, 59.

[5] Edwin Eames and Judith G. Goode, *Anthropology of the City* (Englewood Cliffs, N.J.: Prentice-Hall, 1977), p. 214.

[6] Vella-Kottarathil Roberts, "The Urban Mission of the Church From an Urban Anthropological Perspective" (D.Miss. dissertation, Fuller Theological Seminary, 1981), p. 26.

[7] Wilfred Funk, *Word Origins* (New York: Bell, 1978), pp. 97–98.

[8] Eames and Goode, *Anthropology of the City,* p. 55.

[9] *Philadelphia Inquirer* (5 June 1974): 1F, 4F.

[10]Quoted in Henry J. Schmidt, "The Urban Ethos: Building Churches in a Pagan Environment," *Mission Focus* 8, no. 2 (June 1980): 25.

[11]James L. Spates and John J. Macionis, *The Sociology of Cities* (New York: St. Martin's, 1982), pp. 39–47. Compare "Sociological Contributions to an Urban Anthropology," in *Anthropology of Urban Environments,* ed. Douglas White and Thomas Weaver (Washington: Society for Applied Anthropology, 1972), pp. 97–102.

[12]"Anthropological Approaches to Urban and Complex Society," in White and Weaver, *Anthropology of Urban Environments,* p. 110.

[13]Richard G. Fox, *Urban Anthropology* (Englewood Cliffs, N.J.: Prentice-Hall, 1977), pp. 10–12. For a full survey of the discussion, consult Ulf Hannerz, *Exploring the City* (New York: Columbia University Press, 1980), pp. 76–91.

[14]A full history of this process is available in: Harvie M. Conn, *Eternal Word and Changing Worlds: Theology, Anthropology and Mission in Trialogue* (Grand Rapids: Zondervan, 1984).

[15]For a good summary of Weber's views, consult Herbert F. Hahn, *The Old Testament in Modern Research* (Philadelphia: Fortress, 1966), pp. 159–65.

[16]Don C. Benjamin, *Deuteronomy and City Life* (Washington: University Press of America, 1983), pp. 39–40.

[17]Ibid., p. 47.

[18]Ronald D. Pasquariello, Donald W. Shriver, Jr., and Alan Geyer, *Redeeming the City: Theology, Politics and Urban Policy* (New York: Pilgrim, 1982), p. 17.

[19]Compare Harvie M. Conn, "Christ and the City," in Greenway, *Discipling the City,* pp. 275–76.

[20]Benjamin, *Deuteronomy and City Life,* p. 305.

[21]Frank S. Frick, *The City in Ancient Israel* (Missoula, Mont.: Scholar's Press, 1977), pp. 230–31.

[22]A sample of this difficulty in breaking away from the "theories of contrast" is evident in Benjamin Tonna, *A Gospel for the Cities* (Maryknoll, N.Y.: Orbis, 1982), pp. 29–30. Tonna recognizes in these theories the negative effect of creating "a myth of the village." But he himself does not always escape the myth, as I illustrate in "Christ and the City: A Review Article," *Urban Mission* 1, no. 2 (November 1983): 26–27.

[23]William C. McLaughlin, *Modern Revivalism: Charles Grandison Finney to Billy Graham* (New York: Ronald Press, 1955), p. 166.

[24]Paul Boyer, *Urban Masses and Moral Order in America, 1820-1920* (Cambridge: Harvard University Press, 1978), p. 136. Compare also Robert D. Cross, ed., *The Church and the City 1865-1910* (Indianapolis: Bobbs-Merrill, 1967), pp. xxvi-xxviii.

[25] Francis Schaeffer, *Death in the City* (Downers Grove, Ill.: InterVarsity, 1969), p. 20.

[26] J. H. Bavinck draws out these contradictions in more biblical detail in *The Church Between the Temple and the Mosque* (Grand Rapids: Wm. B. Eerdmans, 1982), pp. 117–27.

[27] Thomas Bender, *Toward an Urban Vision* (Baltimore: John Hopkins University Press, 1975), p. 7.

[28] Carl S. Dudley, *Where Have All Our People Gone?* (New York: Pilgrim, 1979), p. 22.

[29] Fred Graham, *The Constructive Revolutionary* (Atlanta: John Knox, 1971).

[30] John Piet, *The Road Ahead: A Theology for the Church in Mission* (Grand Rapids: Wm. B. Eerdmans, 1970), p. 20.

[31] Gibson Winter, *The Suburban Captivity of the Church* (Garden City, N.Y.: Doubleday, 1961), p. 50.

[32] Graham, *The Constructive Revolutionary,* pp. 97–115.

[33] Dudley, *Where Have All Our People Gone?* p. 21.

[34] Hunter, *American Evangelicalism: Conservative Religion and the Quandary of Modernity,* p. 51.

[35] Ibid., pp. 49–50.

[36] Walter L. Williams, *Black Americans and the Evangelization of Africa, 1877–1900* (Madison: University of Wisconsin Press, 1982); Sylvia M. Jacobs, ed., *Black Americans and the Missionary Movement in Africa* (Westport, Conn.: Greenwood, 1982).

Chapter Two

The Depersonalization
Misunderstanding: "In the City
I'm a Number, Not a Person"

Chapter Two

The Depersonalization
Misunderstanding: "In the City
I'm a Number, Not a Person"

Babylon was one of the first urban development projects recorded in the Bible. Its architects planned it as "the gate of the gods" (Gen. 11:4). It ended as the place of confusion, the epitome of noncommunication (Gen. 11:7–9).

The pressures of technology and industrialization have warped that fact of history into a prooftext for too large a generalization—the city as a synonym for failure, dispersion, powerless dreams.

To a white resident of the United States, the city is the ghetto. And "ghetto" is no longer a sixteenth-century word for that part of Venice where the Jewish colony lived. It means Harlem, Bedford-Stuyvesant, Watts. It means misery, helplessness, cynicism. It conjures up images of "the lonely crowd." Academic descriptions add their technical vocabulary: psychological aberration, social dislocation, low self-concept, rapid social change, familial disorganization.

The bottom line is said to be depersonalization. "Urban

migrants become culturally displaced persons," writes one Christian commentator. "Coming mostly from close-knit, face-to-face societies, the impersonal atmosphere of the big city produces a terrible loneliness. There is a breakdown of the social ties that formerly gave life its meaning, for families break up and friendships that have endured for generations are severed."[1] Value systems are stripped in the city, and people find themselves nobodies. The North American black calls out, "I been down so long, till down don't bother me." A Korean prostitute takes her own life at the age of twenty-four. Beside her body is a simple note, "Tell me who I am. Who am I?"

The greatest need of the urban poor in Acapulco, Mexico? ". . . to be rescued from feelings of isolation, inferiority and self-contempt. All his life he has been taught he is worthless. . . . His part in life is to be poor and remain poor."[2]

"Anomie" has become almost a sister word to describe the same process. It is that normless no-man's-land where a woman beats her two-year-old child with a leather belt and an eighteen-year-old in Mexico City pimps for his fifteen-year-old sister. George Webber calls it "a condition of life in which the true humanity of the person is denied."[3] It is the agony of the city and its challenge to Christian mission.

Increasingly, depersonalization is used as a motivation for church planting. Donald McGavran sees it as one condition among many conducive to church growth in the city.

> Uprooted and transplanted immigrants, starting life anew in strange surroundings and needing community and friendship, flood into cities. These newcomers are away from the close control of family and intimates. . . . They are easily reached.[4]

A massive study of Latin American church growth, done in 1969, repeats the same themes. Urban industrial development is disintegrating traditional Iberian lifestyles. It is accompanied by "depersonalization of life, alteration of family relationships, and modification of cultural values. . . . The attempt to find norms of behaviour in this new order opens the door to the Evangelical Churches."[5]

The message is repeated about Taiwan. "There is opportunity for accelerated growth in the traditional areas that are becoming modernized and industrialized. . . . It is a fact that the anomie of the city and the loneliness of the people contribute to their being winnable."[6]

GETTING THE FACTS STRAIGHT

How will we judge these generalizations? Many qualifiers need to be added to keep reality from slipping into legend. And when the qualifications are all made, our conclusion is this: Urbanization does not always lead to the breakdown of our humanness. Nor does it necessarily promote social instability or normlessness. Life is not that simple. Nor is the city that difficult.

1. Have we started on the wrong foot? Recent urban scholarship is reminding us that "cityness" is a relative thing. Earlier theories, as we saw in chapter 1, relied heavily on a sharp contrast between rural and urban. Many of these formulations in turn depended on the definitions provided by Louis Wirth of the Chicago school, with his heavy accent on population density and size.

Contemporary scholars warn that the terms "rural" and "urban" (and their more technical counterparts) color our understanding of the movement into the city. They introduce an unnecessary and misleading polarization.[7] Urban anthropologists more recently are looking at the connections between cities and outlying communities. Cities are being seen more and more as essential cogs in a worldwide network that stretches to the rural area.[8] They are not closed systems or tightly bound, self-enclosed worlds.

Given this earlier mentality, we tend to focus all our attention on rural-urban migration as a "once-and-only" movement. We forget the links that the urban migrant keeps with the rural homeland. One rural community in Hong Kong, for example, was almost entirely dependent on remittances from emigrants to London. Employed in London restaurants, these migrants sent much of their earnings back to support families in Hong Kong. Despite the distance between London and Hong Kong, there is regular and sometimes frequent visiting.[9] In La Paz, Bolivia, migrants form associations to lobby for schools and higher political status for home communities. West African tribal groups create urban-based voluntary associations to enhance the rural homelands. Apparently the custom of retaining property rights in the village by those individuals who leave is widely practiced in Mexico. In Tilantongo, Mexico, perhaps a third of the migrants still own land in the community.[10]

2. How uprooted is the migrant in reality? The white North Americans who look out of a car window at the graffiti and trash in America's inner cities and hear the late evening news in a suburban home are in great danger. They are primed to shape opinions of city lifestyles on the basis of street and surface appearances. They see cities as disintegrating. They write gospel songs about "lonely cities" and worry about the disappearance of family life. And if they think beyond the United States and Canada, they make the same assumptions about city life in the rest of the world. We are said to be losing our identity in the city, our links with family, our roots.

Those acquainted with migration to the city are saying no to these assumptions more and more loudly. In Madras, India, castes do not often migrate as individuals but as groups. Carolina Carlossi, writing about the Peruvian migrant to the city, comments,

> The caricature of the frightened, confused peasant, belongings under his arm, facing an alien urban environment, is no longer accurate. Most arriving immigrants are quickly absorbed into a supporting web of social relationships.[11]

The migrants do not leave their family structures behind. The presence of relatives in the city may be a prime factor in moving there. The choice of destination and routes taken is often heavily influenced by the presence of friends and relatives. Young women living in intolerable situations of family violence more easily muster the courage to leave if they know they have an aunt or cousin in the city who will take them in. The family will help them find housing and a job. So they go to neighborhoods where people from their own Andean region have settled. The community they move into acquires the characteristics of an extended family that can always find room for one more cousin.[12]

The city, in other words, does not destroy Andean culture or lifestyle. "Andean culture is actually reaffirmed in the city and given new value in the face of urban ridicule."[13]

The myth of the city as a place where family ties are broken needs debunking. The community factor is not missing as much as we have been led to believe in the past.

North American cities display these same patterns. The "urban anonymity" thesis of Louis Wirth doesn't conform to reality. William F. Whyte's *Street Corner Society,* an in-depth study of an Italian immigrant area in an eastern city, appeared in 1943, revealing the existence of strong family, neighborhood, and friendship ties. In the ethnic areas of America's cities, such ties are as intense and intimate as any uncovered in rural areas. Cambodians and Vietnamese "boat people" find their way to their own ethnic neighborhoods in Philadelphia. Ethiopian refugees in Washington, D.C., live in the same areas, setting up ethnic restaurants and businesses, large numbers sharing the same room or house until they can move out on their own.

Perhaps the most powerful testimony to the staying power of the family system in the American city remains the black culture. Devastated by the legacy of slavery, the black family moved northward to the cities in the years following World War I. There the community faced another variety of oppression. And "again the black extended family often cushioned the cruel social environment and made psychic as well as physical survival possible."[14] New forms of togetherness reinforced the family as a "survival mechanism." Large families often adopt more children on an informal basis. Because of shortages in housing and the high cost of living, many people from small towns move into the same house or apartment. In a hostile urban setting, blacks pool their resources and develop a sense of belonging in the creation of surrogate families. Most black churches assume the character of a large extended family.[15]

3. How lonely is the crowd in reality? Is it true that "the loneliest place in the world is not a desolate canyon but a crowded city"?[16] What of the people living in the apartment world of Hong Kong, the condominiums and high-rises of Miami and San Francisco? Earlier theories supposed that loneliness is a fact. As the number of people in social contact became larger, it was supposed that relationships would become thinner, distributed more broadly. And the end would be greater "impersonality."

But research is discovering other answers. In fact, it may well be that the urbanist has moved to the city to find a cure for loneliness. People in apartments, high-rises, and condominiums may not know their neighbors. And they may move into such buildings to maintain their personal privacy. But this does not mean that they do not have personal relationships. They just find them in other channels.

> What seems to be significant about the urban environment is not the lack of ties of attachment but how these ties *vary*. That is, cities seem to encourage *alternative* types of relationships more than other environments do.[17]

Harvey Cox tells in his book *The Secular City* of the shock felt by some Protestant ministers after conducting a survey in a new, urban high-rise apartment area. They expected to encounter lonely people desperate for relationships. In their place they found people who "did not want to meet their neighbors socially and had no interest whatever in church or community groups."[18] They had hoped to develop a kind of village togetherness among people. But instead they found that one of the main reasons people expressed for moving to apartments was to escape the relationships enforced on them by the lack of anonymity of the village. The urban apartment dwellers were seeking lives in which relationships could be founded on free selection and interests other than geographical proximity.

So even the most "private" urban dwellers usually have meaningful relationships. Friendships and intimacies are cultivated. But they are not necessarily local and shaped by geographical proximity as in the village. They are shaped by other considerations—people who work at the same place or who share common interests and recreations. And they are mirrored in the proliferation of urban voluntary associations. There are film societies, singles' bars, karate clubs, health and natural food centers, neighborhood town watches, consciousness-raising groups of all kinds. Homogeneous units are formed to meet human needs for warmth and companionship.

The pattern seems to be worldwide. New social networks are created everywhere, not necessarily connected strictly with the family or along kinship lines. Mass migrations from Europe to the United States in the nineteenth century led to a proliferation of voluntary associations of all kinds. Groups were formed to assist the urban newcomer with mutual aid, medical help, ethnic consciousness, and political awareness.

Peru in particular has provided scholars with abundant information about this kind of voluntary association. Research since the 1950s has investigated occupational clubs, sports clubs, drinking clubs, and professional clubs. The social clubs organized around a locality are continuing to grow; there are clubs representing different villages in almost every town and city in Peru. In Lima, for example, migrants from the remotest Andean villages form regional clubs that offer a place to gather and feel at home in their new surroundings. The clubs serve as buffers that cushion the impact of urban life on recently arrived migrants. They provide newcomers with a familiar environment. They promote hometown improvements and modernization of their original communities.[19] In 1957 there were two hundred such associations in Lima; by 1984, more than six thousand.

On a smaller scale, community develops and networks are created on the street corners in the inner-city ghettos of North America. Elliot Liebow describes the process in *Tally's Corner,* his classic study of black street-corner "losers." Burdened by low self-esteem, hating the work that comes and quickly goes, an evident failure to his wife and children, the black created his own world on the corner. Here failures were rationalized into phantom successes. And weaknesses were magically transformed into successes, through "walking buddies" and girlfriends.[20] On the corner by the carry-out store, losers became winners.

> So important a part of daily life are these relationships that it seems like no life at all without them. Old Mr. Jenkins climbed out of his sick-bed to take up a seat on the Coca-Cola case at the Carry-out for a couple of hours. "I can't stay home and play dead," he explained. "I got to get out and see my friends."[21]

The street corner has become a sanctuary of community.

4. Does the city really cripple personal well-being? Early theorists of the city such as Robert Park and Louis Wirth saw urban size and disorder eating away at mental health and creating what came to be called "urban malaise"—loneliness, depression, and anxiety. Again, the reality may be more hopeful than the generalization.

In 1972 an in-depth study of Manhattan residents pointed the other way. Some 1,660 New Yorkers were questioned in the 1950s; 695 of the same group were surveyed again in the 1970s. The results? The mental health of New Yorkers was slightly better than that of the country residents. In fact, the mental health had improved dramatically over the interval between the two samples, especially for women.[22] A survey taken later by the National Center for Health Statistics reinforced the conclusion. The survey sought to find the incidence of stress-related, chronic health problems, such as hypertension and heart disease, among people over sixty-five. It disclosed such problems in 47.8 per 100 farm residents, 47.5 for small-town residents, and 40.5 for city residents.[23]

Why, then, have so many viewed urban crowding and high population density as leading to behavioral decline? A large part of the problem may be the way in which people's social backgrounds create presuppositions, the spectacles through which we define the data. Upper-middle-class populations, for example, have been socialized to view crowding as a problem. Space and separateness are seen by this social level as natural and necessary. But working-class populations regard the facts differently. Residents of city neighborhoods view high density as a positive sign of community vitality. Contact with others is positive, a sign of belonging, not a sign of crowding. Inner-city children are more comfortable being with others than being alone. Because of this, social workers in the West End of Boston were forced to abandon an experimental summer program that gave inner-city boys a chance to spend a vacation exploring nature on Cape Cod. The boys could not understand why anyone would want to visit, much less live in, such a lonely spot. Wide vistas and open, unused space was, for them, not being where the action was.[24]

Are these cultural blinders the reason why books with titles like *Knowing God* have covers of sunsets and Rocky Mountain vistas, rather than pictures of city children playing in streams of water from a fire hydrant in the summer? Or why devotional guides to prayer and Bible study portray a person on a wooded hillside under a tree and not on a front stoop, with neighbors playing stick ball on the street? How much space do we need to make God real in our lives? Don't churches grow faster where there are more people, not less?

5. *Is the city really more dehumanizing than the country?* This generalization about the depersonalization of the urban process assumes the quality of life is better in the village and in rural life. But is it?

As we noted in chapter 1, Robert Redfield, the father of urban anthropology, answered that question with a strong affirmative. His 1930 study of Tepoztlan, Mexico, painted the village community in an idyllic and Romantic fashion. Midway on the continuum between the folk (primitive) society and the urban society, the village lifestyle is good and pure. There is a strong sense of belonging together. Relations are personal; people are treated as people rather than as things. The members of the community are in intimate contact with one another. Norms, values, and beliefs make the folk society a community of the sacred. There is no place for the entirely secular motive of commercial gain.

By contrast, Redfield continued, are the cities. They are artificial, corrupt, dehumanized, and rational. Impersonality and secularity characterize their lifestyle, anomie their perception of reality.

Redfield's generalizations were challenged in 1951 when Oscar Lewis published his *Life in a Mexican Village: Tepoztlan Restudied.* It was a classic debate that Redfield lost. Lewis raised serious questions about the legitimacy of Redfield's methods and about his rural/village/urban generalizations.[25] He saw village life filled with tensions and feuds. Interpersonal relations were commonly distrustful. There was suspicion, envy, and violence. The village had lost its idealistic rosy hue.

In the ensuing discussion it became apparent the two anthropologists were asking very different questions. Redfield had asked himself what were the things Tepoztecans enjoyed about life. Lewis was more interested in their problems and sufferings. But Lewis was to reinforce his own judgments with field work among the poor migrants of Mexico City. And the earlier judgments about city life appeared more and more as overgeneralized ideals that were not typical. Life in the lower-class neighborhoods of Mexico City had not suffered from disorganization. Social life was not a mass phenomenon. The small groups continued, within the family, within the households, within the neighborhoods. Religious life was not secularized; in fact, it became more Catholic and disciplined. Family networks were not as large as in the village. But they had strengthened and increased. Urban life could hardly be called anonymous and impersonal.[26]

More recent studies on African urban life confirm Lewis's affirmations. Urban Africa "is not wrought with anxiety, stress, and conflict."[27] A 1960 study notes that, considering the way in which urbanization occurred in Africa, a high degree of social disorganization and maladjustment might be expected. The authors conclude, however, "that the extent of adjustment to urban life has been astonishing."[28] There is, to be sure, the culture shock of a shift from rural to urban life. But culture shock is not the same as psychic or social stress.

A CHRISTIAN RESPONSE TO THE REALITIES

All these data should be enough to warn against some of the generalizations made in the past about the city. And they should warn us also against church-planting strategy based on the generalizations. We are encouraged to plant churches in newer working-class neighborhoods because they are "receptive areas." What makes them receptive?

> The typical *barriada* dweller is a man bereft of the ancient values that once sustained him and his family in the rural community where he lived before he migrated to the anonymous and depersonalizing city. He naturally looks forward to a religion in which he can either renew or relive his old values.[29]

Is he really that bereft of the old values? Is the city really that anonymous and depersonalizing? Is he really looking that earnestly for a new religion? Our study says, don't be too sure.

Others plead for urban church planting because the rural-urban links will not last forever. For the time being, we are told, large numbers of the city dwellers are at heart villagers. However, the argument continues, "this come-and-go business is a transitional phenomenon. Larger and larger numbers are becoming permanent residents of the city—as in the West, they never return to their rural solitudes."[30] Is it really that transitional? Studies of Southern Hemisphere countries seem to point elsewhere.

None of this is intended to deflate our Christian hope for church planting in the city. A 1969 study of Latin America hailed that continent's widespread movement to the city as "more likely to render people responsive to the gospel than to make them resistant."[31] We agree. "The areas of urban expansion," the study continued, "are uniquely open to the Evangelical message."

No one has yet made a careful study of the rate of church growth in cities compared with rural areas in Latin America. But we believe the results will confirm the judgments of these three pioneer strategists for the area. How will we see it happen?

1. Rural/urban/suburban networking. The links between so-called Third World rural and urban areas are strong. Already these links have produced urban congregations as Christians drawn to Christ in their rural homelands have moved to the cities and have planted churches there. Some observers in Brazil, for example, suggest that 70 percent of the Presbyterian increase in the cities there has come from Christians moving to town and not from new conversions. Corresponding figures for Baptists are estimated at 50 percent and for Pentecostals, 30 percent.

Timothy Monsma judges that "in Africa the majority are converted *before* they move to the city."[32] Transfer growth cannot be despised, he argues, for the failure of urban churches to grow through transfers of membership would be tragic. It would indicate that many professing Christians are falling away from the faith. That they are not gives us one more reason for doubting the negative impact of the city.

Yet there is continuing evidence of conversions in the city.

Monsma, for example, acknowledges that a majority of the present members of urban Tiv churches in Nigeria were baptized in the rural areas, but it is a slim majority; 48 percent of the men and 45.5 percent of the women members were baptized in the city. And what is the principal instrument in this urban movement? First, web movements, in which the gospel moves through an extended family over a period of years; and second, kinship networking, in which non-Christian relatives travel in a great wave to the city, are housed and helped by Christian kin, and are introduced to the gospel. The networks are not destroyed in the shift from the village to the city. "Detribalization" is a misleading term to describe the African setting. It could equally be called "retribalization," an urban crisscrossing of tribe and class, along whose lines the gospel is still carried.

The significance of these roots and links needs to be explored in terms of church growth. They provide exciting possibilities for reaching cities. In Africa, for example,

> people who move to the city seek out members of their own tribe for this gives them a sense of security and identity in the midst of change. Many new urbanites plan to retire to their tribal area someday, and they do not want to lose their tribal identity. The church can capitalize on this thirst for tribal identity by offering church services in tribal languages and fellowship among those who think alike. In the cities of northern Nigeria there are always at least two Anglican congregations, each with its own church building, one for the Yoruba migrants and one for the Ibo people. In this way the Anglicans preserve denominational unity while providing tribally oriented congregations, and they are today the largest Protestant communion in Nigeria. The Anglican experience may well serve as a model for others to follow.[33]

North American missionaries, insensitive to this rural-to-urban kin networking, must learn to recognize it. Should they be encouraged to spend the first five years on the field in a rural area known for its heavy migration patterns to the city? Then, building on the relationships created by those years of association with family and tribe, move to the city in the same invasion wave of migrants? They have identified with the source of the stream. They will be all the more at home in the new wave to the city. The missionary outsider has became an insider-in-process along with other rural outsiders.

Similarly, how can we make use of the back-and-forth passage of the migrant between city and village? If church planting is possible on one end of the rural–urban continuum, why is it not also possible on the other? Urban migrants keep their ties with the rural homeland: what significance does this have for church growth? Studies of return migrants (of whatever duration) in Vicos, Peru, in the fifties and sixties saw them

> as less conservative than those who had had little or no contact with people outside their natal place; they are also more receptive to innovations. As such they may act as cultural brokers or mediators between the urban and rural sectors or the national and local systems.[34]

What function could they perform if, having roots in the homeland, they carried back with them the gospel that had wooed and won them in the city? Could the potential change agent for the village be also a transcultural broker for the kingdom of God? A mentality that builds on a radical break between the rural and the urban may be missing a "bridge of God" in either locale.

Is this part of the reason why the work of the Conservative Baptist Foreign Mission Society of North America has not grown as it might in Uganda, East Africa? By 1972 the CBFMS had six churches in Kampala, the capital city. Their conviction was that "if effective evangelism was able to permeate the cities, Christianity automatically would spread to the rural areas."[35] But by 1982, when this author visited Kampala, there was only one congregation left in the city, with no strong growth of the churches in the rural areas. Why? Assuredly, one cannot forget the devastating effect of Idi Amin's holocaust on the life of Uganda and its churches. Nor can we dismiss some concern over the spiritual strength of the churches and their leadership. But are these factors the major reasons for the church's decimation? Should we not look to strategy issues?

Was it the assumption in Uganda that the gospel would "automatically" flow from the city to the villages? Was it the choice of the missionaries to work in the Luganda language in Kampala while rural work was going ahead among the Banyar-wanda-speaking peoples of the Masaka area? The rural-urban continuum had been minimized by choosing to work with separate cultural, kin groupings on either end of the pipeline. And what effect did it have with five missionary families in Kampala and only one in the Masaka area? The city was being viewed primarily as a container, not a channel.

"Networking" in North American cities must take a different shape. Here the continuum flows, not between rural and urban, but between urban and suburban. And the flow is clogged by the "white flight" that has sent formerly urban white churches to the suburbs in the face of growing black and ethnic communities that have reshaped the cities in the last three decades. White racism adds a new demand to networking in American cities—the demands of reconciliation and repentance for emptied urban church buildings and lost evangelistic opportunities.

Institutions have arisen conscious of these responsibilities and seeking to be bridge builders between white suburban churches and minority fellowships. Emmanuel Gospel Center, opened in Boston in 1964 under the direction of Douglas Hall, has seen "resource networking" as a major part of its task. By making its facilities available to urban ministries, it has become involved in the planting of a score of churches. As a communications system, it helps to meet the informational needs of urban churches and ministries across the country. It seeks to establish links with persons and ministries that have common interests and concerns as they minister in the urban environment. A "Love-In-Action" program networks information about Boston area ministries and their needs to the broader Christian community. The center encourages the establishment of social concern components in local churches and provides concrete answers to the question, "What can we do?" Its published catalogue of churches and ministries provides help in referral, finding resources, and networking models of various urban ministries with each other. It has established links with Gordon-Conwell Theological Seminary and provides an urban middler year of study for its largely suburban constituency.[36]

In Philadelphia, the Center for Urban Theological Studies (CUTS) fulfills a similar role. Begun at the urging of the city's black pastors, it has developed from its natal days in 1971 and its early associations with Westminster Theological Seminary into an independent program supported and owned by a constituency of black, Hispanic, Korean, and suburban churches. Its study programs bring together leaders in the urban churches with pastors and students from the suburban, white communities and with missionaries serving in the Third World. The center's emphasis on racial reconciliation becomes what the founder and director, Bill Krispin, calls the "hidden curriculum." CUTS has played a formative role in the creation of the Philadelphia Ministries Coalition, a consortium of congregations drawing its leadership from all the ethnic spectrum of the city and spearheading the development of interracial Christian ministry to the city. It remains committed to the interdependence of suburb and city.

2. Evangelism in the rite-of-passage period. Anthropologists often speak of rites of passage. These are rituals used to mark the occasions in life when individuals or groups move from one life status to another, such as baptism, a graduation exercise, or marriage. During the 1960s in the United States, long hair for some teenage boys became virtually a ritual symbol of rejection of their parents' authority. The rituals symbolize the crossing of a cultural threshold, the disintegration of an old way of life, and the passage into a new one. That period of time (called "liminal") midway between the two cultural worlds is crucial.

Are we stretching the language too far if we describe the passage of the migrant from a rural to an urban setting in similar terms? The period of time between the discarding of rural ways and the putting on of the urban becomes a liminal passage, a time of cultural dislocation and anomie. There is uncertainty, concern, and even fear. It is a time of special vulnerability and openness to new ways. At this point of transition, the fledgling urbanite is truly uprooted.

It is in this circumstance that evangelism may be the most fruitful. The gospel can become, under the leadership of the Holy Spirit, a functional substitute for a rite of passage. Thus Donald McGavran wisely notes that "one group which should normally prove receptive is that made up of recent rural immigrants who have come permanently to the city—especially if they have come from overseas."[37]

Is this the reason why the church in Japan has grown scarcely at all in the villages? The growth that has occurred has come from converted city dwellers. And in Brazil great migrations from the poverty of the northeast have been exciting sources of growth in the cities to the south.

Is this why it is safe to say that a newer city is usually more receptive than an older city, and a growing city is usually more receptive than a static or declining one? Howard Snyder affirms this of the Free Methodist Church in Brazil.

> The most obviously responsive people in São Paulo are those who live in the new communities that form the growing edge of the urban area. The most effective, least difficult church planting is done by starting new congregations in new areas that are only 20 to 50 per cent inhabited. . . . It is in such areas that we have had the most success.[38]

The United States provides illustrations, both sad and glorious, of this kind of opportunity in the years following World War I. Racial turnover of its center-city areas began as the great migration of blacks out of the rural South began. The pull of northern industrial jobs in the city, the boll weevil's destruction of cotton and the mechanization of agriculture, white hostility and inhumanity—all combined to cause 400,000 blacks to go north between 1910 and 1920.

The resurgence of industry during World War II accelerated the pace, and it continued into the 1950s and 1960s. Mississippi's black population declined more than 100,000 during the 1960s. By the 1970s, Chicago housed more blacks than all of Mississippi. The New York metropolitan area had more blacks than any state of the Old South. It was a massive rural-to-urban movement.

Blinded by the glow of the suburbs and fear of the black arrival, the white evangelical churches moved to the edges of the city and forsook a marvelous opportunity for harvesting. Presbyterians abandoned two churches in the city for every one they organized in the suburbs.[39] A whole culture was in the process of passage from rural to urban—and the white churches fled from the scene.

On the other hand, the black church moved with its people. The established black churches of the North could not absorb the flood of newcomers. Often too ritualistic and formal in worship style, they could not meet the cultural demands of the southern blacks; but the void was filled by the mobility of storefront churches. And there were new churches, some Baptist and some Pentecostal, with deep roots in the southern tradition, that moved north to meet the needs and experience new growth. The black churches were there at the right time. They crossed the passage from rural to urban cultures with their people.

3. *Building Christian community appropriate for the city.* City life, we have learned, is not based on shallow, impersonal ties between people. The primary networks of kin and family and tribe do not slowly disappear. And for that reason, it is still good advice to "multiply tribe, caste, and language churches" in the city. Cities are not "melting pots," the separate ethnic ingredients of the stew eventually dissolving into the whole. Rather, they are "salad

bowls," with each ingredient in the salad contributing to the whole, yet not losing its identity.

But in the city other networking links become part of the integrative process. The large-scale dimension of the city promotes these. In America, people build community in front of inner-city carry-out stores or at bars catering to singles or to homosexuals. Common neighborhood needs—shortage of water, poor housing, child care—draw people to one another. Social networks are not destroyed by the city; new ones are created, not always connected strictly with family or kin.

Church-planting methods must take these facts into consideration. But this does not always happen easily. We continue to think in geographical categories in the city, around concepts of a "parish" created for a rural setting. A more functional definition of proximity is necessary for innovative urban church growth. The Lausanne Committee suggests,

> The urban church cannot define its evangelism too narrowly. Failure to work with, and in, those secondary systems can result in an urban environment which becomes a barrier to effective evangelism. For example, involvement with the concerns of the poor (housing, employment, etc.), and the victims of institutional injustice are central to reaching such people with a holistic message of hope and salvation.[40]

In Sydney, Australia, a "Church in the Market Place" has developed to meet these functional needs of the city. Planted in the center of the commercial development in the eastern suburbs, it concentrates on providing deep human companionship and the discovery of talents to set people free to contribute to society. It has set up schools for senior citizens in its search for providing growth opportunities for those whom it sees as hopeless. It serves in community aid and child care and ministers through a girls' hostel. It exists to reach out, worship, pray, and care.

In Seoul, Korea, in the 1970s a growing number of singers and actors, producers, directors, and writers in the entertainment world came to Christ. Bound together by their profession, and troubled by the notoriety that might accompany them if they attached themselves to local churches, they had formed their own fellowship by the end of the decade. A church made up of professional athletes has also formed out of similar circumstances in Korea's capital.

Earlier we spoke of the rapid growth of voluntary associations and clubs in Peru. Formed during the semi-permanent and early stages of migration to act as a buffer, the clubs are often short-lived because of declining need for them. Other associations take their place and become small social and recreational groups. The migrants find that they need these associations less and less as they become more adapted to the city. Should not church and missionary be building links with these clubs during the crucial time of ministry to the new migrants? In a time ripe with evangelistic opportunity, the club becomes an institutional rite of passage between the rural and the urban milieus. How can the gospel piggyback on this transitional organization?

Creative adaptations to similar urban networks are appearing in Singapore. Seventy percent of the population live in high-rise apartments. The church has risen to the challenge. House churches have been initiated in New States (50,000 to 200,000 people) where as recently as 1980 there was no corporate Christian presence. Christian residents are identified, then brought together for Bible study, worship, and evangelism. In the meantime, the central business district is not forgotten. In this area, where a half-million people work, a number of Christians have formed small groups, meeting six days a week, in almost every building. There is no organizational focus. All are spontaneous, with urban professionals running their own groups. While this is going on, industrial workers as a "hidden people" still wait to be discovered.[41]

   4. *Overcoming frustration with hope and optimism.* Behind past generalizations of the city as a depersonalizing force may lie hidden the most dangerous myth of all—frustration and despair over the

possibility of church growth, an urban fatigue that calls for a theology of failure.

Even the invigorating optimism of Donald McGavran seems to fade in regard to cities. The chapter in his magnum opus on "discipling urban populations" is filled with sentences such as, "After a hundred and fifty years of modern missions, the plain fact is that churches have not done well in most cities of Africasia." Or he adds sadly, "Failure of the Church to grow in most cities is not due to lack of effort." Or, in a sentence that needs correction, he asserts, "In the United States and Canada, churches have multiplied in new suburbs among native-born white Protestant populations, but have declined in inner cities [sic] and in 'changing neighborhoods.'" He says all this as part of his urgent call for researching urban church growth, a need that has yet to be fulfilled nearly two decades after he penned these words in 1970. Almost the last words he writes in the chapter urge us on: "Discipling urban populations is perhaps the most urgent task confronting the Church."[42] But the optimism is dimmed.

Abraham had God's verbal guarantee that if Sodom had as few as ten righteous people, God would spare the city (Gen. 18:32). What will He say to Seoul, Korea, which had 2,500 churches in 1980? Or Pusan in the same country with 1,103? Or Lahore, Pakistan, with 45?

When the children of Israel were about to end forty years as a rural, nomadic people and possess the land of Canaan, God encouraged them to see the cities they would now occupy as gifts from Him (Deut. 6:10–12). Does our vision of the city see it as divine gift, or human nightmare?

His unfolding plan of salvation for the nations enfolds the cities by His grace. Even the inhabitants of Babylon will be given citizenship papers stating, "This one was born in Zion" (Ps. 87:4, 6). The urban empires of Egypt and Assyria will hear the words of the Lord, "Blessed be Egypt my people, Assyria my handiwork, and Israel my inheritance" (Isa. 19:25). Damascus will be restored to its place within the boundaries of the people of God (Ezek. 47:16–18).

The work of the coming Messiah will be urban work: "God will save Zion and rebuild the cities of Judah" (Ps. 69:35). The town crier who brings good tidings is to go to a high mountain and lift up his voice with a shout: "Say to the cities of Judah, 'Here is your God!' See, the Sovereign LORD comes with power" (Isa. 40:9–10). One day God will fulfill the word He speaks of the cities of Judah: "They shall be built" (Isa. 44:26).

These words of prophecy are not the careless words of overdone optimism. The New Testament stamps them as sure, fulfilled affirmations of hopes accomplished. Jesus comes to "preach the good news of the kingdom of God to the other cities also" (Luke 4:43). He commissions His seventy to announce the beginning of the eschatological harvest day of God (Luke 10:2; cf. Joel 3:13–16; Amos 9:13). They are sent "to every city and place where He was going to come" (Luke 10:1). The ruined cities are being rebuilt by the word of grace from the Messiah (Amos 9:14). The banquet servants of the Lord are being commissioned to invite passersby to the feast. Where do they go? "Into the streets and lanes of the city" (Luke 14:21). And what shall be the reward of faithful stewards of kingdom talents? "Enter into the joy of the Lord," says the master in Matthew 25:21. In Luke 19, the joy of the Lord has become cities: "Because you have been trustworthy in a very small matter, take charge of ten cities" (v. 17).

The triumphant march of Jesus and His people through the world becomes a march through cities in the Book of Acts. "A city of Samaria" rejoices in the gospel message of Philip, and the Word of the Lord begins to break out of its Jewish container (Acts 8:5, 8). In Caesarea a Roman centurion, Cornelius, is welcomed into a new kind of urban fellowship (Acts 10:24). Damascus, a traditional enemy of Israel, welcomes another enemy, Paul (Acts 9:2), and sends him forth an apostle to the cities. Derbe, Lystra, Thessalonica, Athens, Corinth, Ephesus, and Rome all bow to the power of the gospel.

The Bible ends with the final urban victory. The cities of the nations collapse (Rev. 16:19). Babylon falls, the great urban emblem of immorality and the abominations of the earth (Rev. 17:5); in one hour, doom comes to the city of power (18:10). And before us stand the new heavens and the new earth, not a garden but now a city, "coming down out of heaven from God"; the urban bride has come, "beautifully dressed for her husband" (Rev. 21:2). The kings of the earth come, bringing their splendor to the city of God (Rev. 21:24).

In all this, no room is allowed for despondency and discouragement. We do not lose our humanity in the cities of the world. In Christ it is restored, rebuilt, reshaped. The violence of Cain, the world's first city builder (Gen. 4:17), cannot destroy what we are. The image of God remains an indelible stamp that God protects (Gen. 5:1–2; 9:6). And in the cities of the world Jesus, the perfect image of God (Eph. 4:24), continues to mold them after His likeness (Col. 3:10).

NOTES

[1] Edward Murphy, "Guidelines for Urban Church Planting," in *Crucial Issues in Missions Tomorrow,* ed. Donald A. McGavran (Chicago: Moody, 1972), p. 246.

[2] Tom Courtney, "Mission to the Urban Poor," *Urban Mission* 1, no. 2 (November 1983): 18.

[3] George W. Webber, *The Congregation in Mission* (Nashville: Abingdon, 1964), p. 27.

[4] Donald A. McGavran, *Understanding Church Growth* (Grand Rapids: Wm. B. Eerdmans, rev. ed. 1980), pp. 318–19.

[5] William R. Read, Victor M. Monterroso, and Harmon A. Johnson, *Latin American Church Growth* (Grand Rapids: Wm. B. Eerdmans, 1969), p. 246.

[6] Quoted in Amirtharaj Nelson, *A New Day in Madras* (South Pasadena: William Carey Library, 1975), p. 71. A more detailed but similar conclusion is reached in Robert J. Bolton, *Treasure Island: Church Growth Among Taiwan's Urban Minnan Chinese* (South Pasadena: William Carey Library, 1976), pp. 162–65.

[7] Douglas Butterworth and John K. Chance, *Latin American Urbanization* (Cambridge: Cambridge University Press, 1981), p. 39.

[8] Anthony Leeds, "Towns and Villages in Society: Hierarchies of Order and Cause," in *Cities in a Larger Context,* ed. Thomas W. Collins (Athens: University of Georgia Press, 1980), pp. 6–12.

[9] Edwin Eames and Judith G. Goode, *Anthropology of the City* (Englewood Cliffs, N.J.: Prentice-Hall, 1977), pp. 246–49.

[10] Butterworth and Chance, *Latin American Urbanization,* p. 78.

[11] *Latinamerica Press* (20 September 1984): 4.

[12] Butterworth and Chance, *Latin American Urbanization,* pp. 94–98.

[13] Paul L. Doughty, "Peruvian Migrant Identity in the Urban Milieu," in *The Anthropology of Urban Environments,* ed. Thomas Weaver and Douglas White (Washington: Society for Applied Anthropology, 1972), p. 40.

[14] J. Deotis Roberts, *Roots of a Black Future: Family and Church.* (Philadelphia: Westminster, 1980), p. 79.

[15] Ibid., pp. 88–89.

[16] Mariano DiGangi, "The Church and the Inner City," in *The Urban Crisis,* ed. David McKenna (Grand Rapids: Zondervan, 1969), p. 116.

[17] James L. Spates and John J. Macionis, *The Sociology of Cities* (New York: St. Martin's, 1982), p. 48.

[18] Harvey Cox, *The Secular City* (London: SCM Press, 1965), p. 44.

[19] Butterworth and Chance, *Latin American Urbanization,* p. 139.

[20] Elliot Liebow, *Tally's Corner* (Boston: Little, Brown, 1967), p. xii.

[21] Ibid., p. 164.

[22] Spates and Macionis, *The Sociology of Cities,* p. 54.

[23] Tim Hackler, "The Big City Has No Corner on Mental Illness," *New York Times Magazine* (19 December 1979): 136, 138.

[24] Herbert J. Gans, *Urban Villagers* (Glencoe, Ill.: Free Press, 1962); Gerald Suttles, *The Social Order of the Slum* (Chicago: University of Chicago Press, 1968).

[25] "Anthropological Approaches to Urban and Complex Society," in Weaver and White, *The Anthropology of Urban Environments,* p. 110.

[26] A good summary of the debate will be found in Ulf Hannerz, *Exploring the City* (New York: Columbia University Press, 1980), pp. 59–72.

[27] William J. Hanna and Judith L. Hanna, *Urban Dynamics in Black Africa* (New York: Aldine, 1981), p. 80.

[28] Suzanne Comhaire-Sylvain and Jean L. L. Comhaire, "Problems Relating to Urbanization: Formation of African Urban Populations," in *Population in Africa,* ed. Frank Lorimer and Mark Karp (Boston: Boston University Press, 1960), p. 42.

[29] Quoted in C. Peter Wagner, *Frontiers in Missionary Strategy* (Chicago: Moody, 1971), p. 190.

[30] McGavran, *Understanding Church Growth*, p. 315.

[31] Read, Monterroso, and Johnson, *Latin American Church Growth*, p. 280.

[32] Timothy Monsma, *An Urban Strategy for Africa* (Pasadena: William Carey Library, 1979), p. 46.

[33] Timothy Monsma, "Reaching Africa's Growing Cities," in *Guidelines for Urban Church Planting*, ed. Roger S. Greenway (Grand Rapids: Baker, 1976), p. 69.

[34] Butterworth and Chance, *Latin American Urbanization*, p. 79.

[35] Gailyn Van Rheenen, *Church Planting in Uganda* (South Pasadena: William Carey Library, 1976), p. 93.

[36] Douglas Hall, "Emmanuel Gospel Center, Boston: Contextualized Urban Ministry," *Urban Mission* 1, no. 2 (November 1983): 31–36.

[37] McGavran, *Understanding Church Growth*, p. 316.

[38] Howard A. Snyder, "The Free Methodist Church in São Paulo, Brazil," in Greenway, *Guidelines for Urban Church Planting*, p. 25.

[39] Carl Dudley, "Churches in Changing Communities," in *Metro-Ministry*, ed. David Frenchak and Sharrel Keyes (Elgin, Ill.: David C. Cook, 1979), pp. 78–79.

[40] *Thailand Report—Christian Witness to Large Cities*. Lausanne Occasional Papers, no. 9 (Wheaton, Ill.: Lausanne Committee for World Evangelization, 1980), p. 27.

[41] Ibid., p. 32.

[42] McGavran, *Understanding Church Growth*, p. 352.

Chapter Three

The Crime Generalization: "I'm Afraid of the City"

Chapter Three

The Crime Generalization: "I'm Afraid of the City"

The image of the city for most white North Americans is negative. At an Inter-Varsity Christian Fellowship conference on the city in 1983, Dr. Roger Greenway and I spoke on "Spiritual Values in the Urban Setting." To get the roomful of students thinking, Dr. Greenway asked them, "How would you define a city?" He filled a blackboard with their answers. Eleven characteristics were listed: three positive, eight negative. Words such as "ghetto, crime, stress, anomie, loneliness, loss of individuality, rapid change, loss of personhood" stood out boldly. All added up to pessimism.

Greenway continued his survey. "Religiously," he asked, "what do you find in the city?" The answers were totally negative—apathy and complacence, WASP flight to the suburbs, a religion of money and power, introversion, cults (Jim Jones, Satanism), relativism and pluralism, the occult, moral breakdown, a focus on "just-certain-things and skip-the-rest."

Urban sociology textbooks underscore the pessimism. They

speak of "the urban crisis" instead of "the urban challenge," "urban problems" instead of "urban issues." And the list these texts include seems universal—poverty, housing, crime, mob disorder, unemployment and underemployment, environmental problems, fiscal crisis.

Pessimism breeds fear, and fear seems widespread. A mid-1970s survey indicated that 56 percent of the people (75 percent of the women) living in cities of more than one million were afraid to walk the streets at night in their own neighborhoods.[1]

Out of the siege mentality we speak of police stations in the Bronx, New York, as "Fort Apache." Out of the realities of North America's inner cities we create new vocabulary: *mugging, hustling, ghetto.* "Guardian Angel" used to convey the imagery of heavenly protection and unseen ministries; now it speaks to the American of city subways, karate training, and red berets. Our film heroes used to be rural, the cowboys of the mythical West— John Wayne, Gary Cooper. Now our film heroes have become almost pathological themselves—the vigilante law of Clint Eastwood's *Dirty Harry* or Charles Bronson's *Death Wish.*

Is it any wonder that one of the sociology texts I consulted for this study begins its chapter on urban crisis with the inscription over the gate of hell from Dante's *Divine Comedy?*

> Through me the way into the doleful city,
> Through me the way into eternal grief,
> Through me a people forsake.

Shelley, the English Romantic poet, embodies the same concerns in his epigram, "Hell is a city much like London."

FACTS

It is through the window of the North American city that the cities of the rest of the world are viewed. And those windows are perceived as dirty and broken. An Associated Press national poll released in July 1981 reported 85 percent of Americans were more afraid of crime than they were five years earlier. And *Newsweek* magazine in that same year capsulized the reason for it in the apparent explosion of street crime in urban America.

> They started walking at dusk, two teenagers casually spreading the message that the streets of West Los Angeles were no longer safe. First they stopped Phillip Lerner and demanded money. Lerner had no cash, only his infant in a stroller. They let him pass and kept walking. They hailed Arkady and Rachel Muskin at a nearby intersection. The couple quickly handed over $8 and two wristwatches, and gratefully fled. Next the boys intercepted two elderly Chinese women and pulled out a pistol. When one woman tried to push the gun out of her face, ten bullets blazed out, killing both. The boys kept walking. They came upon a trio of friends out for an evening stroll. They took a watch and a few dollars and, without so much as a word, killed one of the three, a Frenchman visiting Los Angeles for the first time. The boys kept walking. At last they reached a drive-in restaurant where they found 76-year-old Leo Ocon walking on the sidewalk. They argued with him for less than a minute and then shot him down. Their evening over, they climbed into an old sedan and then, much as they had started, calmly went off into the night.[2]

The major source for crime data in the United States remains the Uniform Crime Reports (UCR) of the Federal Bureau of Investigation (FBI). The statistics are frightening reinforcements for suburban concerns about the city. Calculating the crime rate by dividing the number of offenses that police departments report by the total population, the picture seems to be clear.

Violent crime increased 199.3 percent from 1960 to 1975. And by 1975 it was well over three times as prevalent in "metropolitan areas" as in rural ones. Robbery in 1979 was more than ten times as frequent in metropolitan as in rural areas.

Then there are the crimes not reported by the victims. Recent estimates are that the UCR includes only 50 percent of robberies committed; there are 3.5 times as many rapes committed as are reported to police. Automobile thefts are reported 89 percent of the time, burglaries only 58 percent. The conclusion of Alan S. Berger?

> Whatever the source, the evidence seems clear: the larger the city, the higher the rate of violent crime; with the exception of cities over a million, the higher also the rate of property crime. There is considerable evidence that there is something about cities that encourages criminal acts.[3]

To add a future dimension to the fear, crime is said to be an activity of the young. Some 45 percent of crimes excepting murder are committed by people under eighteen. Three-quarters are committed by those under twenty-five. The most likely age for being arrested is sixteen; fifteen-, seventeen-, and eighteen-year-olds come next.[4]

Is it any wonder that Henry Ford, the automobile genius, once said, "We shall solve the City problem by leaving the City"? Or why the elderly, retired couple who sold us our home in urban Philadelphia a few years ago had four chain locks on their front door? Why Henry James described New York as a fifty-floored conspiracy against the idea of the ancient graces? Or why Frank Lloyd Wright, the architect, called city people "selfishly bred, children of pleasure herding on hard, crowded pavements in congested urban areas" and pontificated that "the breed naturally gets the worm's eye view suited to the Cashandcarry mentality"?[5]

People with a knowledge of Third World cities speak, by comparison, of their relative freedom from street crime. Calcutta has an international reputation as the epitome of urban problems— massive overcrowding, flooding, malaria, cholera, a half-million people who live and die without ever sleeping under a roof. Yet it is also the active center of Bengali poetry and theater. And it does not tolerate street crime against women. Indian women in Calcutta can walk even at night with a degree of safety unknown in "Christianized" London or New York. The same could be said of Seoul or Bangkok.

Yet violence and crime bubble to the surface in the Third

World cities also. Medellín, Colombia's second largest city (2.3 million people), has a string of titles: "commercial center of Colombia," "textile king of South America." To it has been added still another: "Colombia's capital of crime." John Maust writes, "Throughout South and Central America, it's common to hear the buck passed for any common crime: 'It was probably a Colombian who did it.' "[6] Drug traffic, Mafia activity, and political terrorism all feed the image. In the first nine months of 1983 there were 679 homicides in Medellín; health officials said homicide might soon pass cancer and heart disease as the city's leading cause of death.

Friends warn visitors to Medellín: Don't walk alone at night; don't carry an exposed camera; watch out for thieves on the buses who will slit your bag and snatch the contents before you know it. Residents put steel bars over their windows, and they cement pieces of jagged glass atop the concrete walls they build to surround their homes. Watchdogs are visible on the roofs. Some say more crimes per capita are committed in Medellín than in any other city in the world, but such a claim is hard to prove.

Drug-related problems multiply the woes of cities everywhere. In São Paulo, a city of 7.5 million, more than 200,000 addicts consume an estimated 80 kilos of cocaine and about a ton of marijuana per month! About 50 percent of Mexico City's population is under the age of fifteen, and drug and alcohol abuse poses severe problems. In Mexico nationally, the National Youth Council (CREA) reports that 75,000 young people drop out of school every year because of alcohol; 3 million youths between the ages of twelve and twenty-five are alcoholics.[7]

Prostitution is said to grow in those places where the population is dense, the poor are numerous, and money flows freely. In one country where these three factors are all found, an estimated 13 percent of the female population of the capital city are reported to be prostitutes.[8] It is estimated that approximately 41 percent of Taiwan's youths between the ages of fifteen and twenty-four are either juvenile delinquents or prostitutes; in Taipei, the capital, the figure reaches 80,000.[9]

The problems grow increasingly among preadolescents. In Latin America, girls most in demand are between the ages of ten and fourteen. A girl aged twenty-two can bring in more money in Brazil than a man can earn by working full-time in a factory. A recent report from Colombo, Sri Lanka, states there are two thousand small boys in prostitution. In the United States there are at least 264 pornographic magazines specializing in child-related sexual activities.

There are packaged sex tours on a large scale in the Caribbean, Southeast Asia, and parts of Africa. INTERPOL, the international police network, has uncovered the existence of a number of multinational combines involved in buying and transporting women and children for sexual exploitation. Poverty, combined with male chauvinism, makes girls available for sale in Macao for $100 or $200.

Violence takes political form in Third World cities through torture and assassinations. "Consensus by repression" becomes part of the new urban power order. Uruguay became a "national security" state in 1973. From that year until 1978, 50,000 citizens were imprisoned and half of them savagely tortured. According to Amnesty International's estimates, one of every 450 people in Uruguay is a Prisoner of Conscience; approximately one of every 50 citizens has suffered interrogation, temporary arrest, or imprisonment.[10] The Argentine record on human rights violations is shattering: 15,000 disappeared during the 1970s; there were 10,000 political prisoners, and 4,000 people were killed for political reasons. In Chile in 1976 the number of persons arrested and never seen again was estimated by Amnesty International at more than 1,500. "It is impossible to know for sure," AI reported, "whether these persons are dead or held incommunicado in camps and prisons. In every case habeas corpus writs presented by their families were rejected."[11]

Fed by the imitation of colonial power manipulation, political power seeking in urbanizing Africa yields to corruption. The hubris of capital cities is fed by what anthropologists call "urban primacy," a condition in which capital cities are overwhelmingly larger than the size of the second city. In Guinea the capital is apparently nine times bigger than the next-largest town; in Senegal, Liberia, and Togo it is nearly seven times larger. To feed the showcase nature of the capital, the political, social, and cultural structures appropriate the wealth and help that should be spread throughout the country. In Abidjan, Ivory Coast, the eight-story, 500-bed Centre Hospitalier Universitaire was built in 1968 as a result of this bias toward the power center. One of the largest and most modern hospitals in Africa, it was erected in the luxurious Cocody quarter, home of high government officials. But the funds for the building, given by France, were originally intended for twelve regional hospitals.[12]

Meanwhile, the contrast between the mansions of the rich and the shacks of the poor grows. The new ruling elite place low budget priority on new urban housing and allocate much of a nation's resources to benefit the already rich. Political power becomes the key both to public authority and to the many goods and services that public institutions produce and distribute. Kwame Nkrumah's adage describes much of Africa's urban-centered political life: "Seek ye first the political kingdom and all things will be added unto you." Crime becomes administrative policy.

Reinforcing this quest for urban power bases are the bruising struggles arising from African tribal rivalries. Ethnic favoritism often affects who gets patronage jobs and building or management contracts and determines which ethnic group will be awarded the use of publicly owned shops and market stalls. Politics is dominated by ethnic membership, creating in its wake patron-client networks that carve up urban resources and power.[13]

> Someone said
> Independence falls like a bull buffalo
> And the hunters
> Rush to it with drawn knives
> Sharp shining knives
> For carving the carcass.

And if your chest
Is small, bony and weak
They push you off,
And if your knife is blunt
You get the dung on your elbow
But come home empty-handed
And the dogs bark at you.[14]

FANCIES

The reality of crime in the urban areas of the United States is difficult to deny. But it does seem that the largely white suburbanites have a fear of city crime out of all proportion to the facts. A national sample taken in 1973 and 1974 found that as many as 36 percent of the people polled in towns of less than 50,000 were afraid to walk alone at night within one mile of their homes.[15]

Part of the fear comes from the cultural definitions of crime that color middle-class perceptions in the West. Crime is often defined in terms of street crime that involves violence. It is also frequently overlaid with racial fears. One critic writes, "It is easily transposed into an ugly kind of wishful thinking: 'If only the blacks [or the Latins or the criminals or whatever] were not here, we would not have any urban problems.'"[16] An "ideology of the suburban haven" seeks to relegate the crime problem to the city.

As a matter of fact, statistical studies offer a confused picture. Few deny that there are higher crime rates in larger cities than in smaller ones, in central cities than in small suburbs. It is equally true that suburban crime tends to be much less violent than city crime. Someone living in the city of Chicago, for instance, is six times more likely to be murdered and seven times more likely to be robbed than a suburban resident.

Yet the suburbs are far from being havens. Since 1970, there is a greater *relative* rise in the crime rates of smaller cities and suburbs. J. John Palen explains, "This can be misleading, though, because the suburban increase is applied to a much smaller [population] base. The amount of crime thus remains smaller. As of 1975, for example, there were 52.1 crimes per 1,000 persons in central cities but only 36.1 in suburbs."[17]

Crime is not a center-city phenomenon. Certain types of crimes, such as alcoholism and drug abuse, occur in all environments. But other kinds of criminal activity, such as "white-collar crime," are concentrated in middle-class and upper-class areas. "In fact," note two writers on urban sociology, "if the white-collar criminal were treated by the criminal justice system in the same manner as the traditional blue-collar criminal, the overall picture of ecological patterning of criminal activity in our nation's cities might be vastly altered. Instead of crime being concentrated in poorer areas of the city, suburban and well-to-do sections would also be seen as housing their share of criminals."[18]

Why is this perception of white-collar crime seen as less frightening? Could it be tied to the "privatization myth" we explore in a subsequent chapter—the difficulty we have defining evil as anything other than an individual act of violation against another individual? Embezzlement, stock fraud, and price fixing are not seen as crimes of coercion against the person. And those captivated by the privatization mythology of sin as only an individual act do not see white-collar crime as threatening to one's well-being in the manner of a mugging or an armed robbery. Through these glasses it is easier to see evil on the street than in the boardroom or shopping mall.

Could it be also that we associate crime—"real" crime—with those features of the city we have regarded in previous chapters? The size of the city, the density of its populations, the ethnic and social heterogeneity of its networks become attributes not demographic so much as primarily anti-moralistic. They become qualitative ways of looking at the city, not simply quantitative. Our bias against the city leads us to *expect* there to be crime in the city.

Urban scholarship has certainly not escaped this bias, as we have seen in the formative work of the Chicago school of thought. More contemporary examples reinforce the view. A 1970 anthropological textbook refers to urbanites as "enslaved by an artificial environment" and sees the city of Timbuctoo in Mali, West Africa, as similar to American urban culture in its money emphasis, crime, cheating, and dishonesty.[19] Let's recall the statement by Alan S. Berger, cited earlier in this chapter, that "there is considerable evidence that there is something about cities that encourages criminal acts." On the page following that statement, Berger offers this illuminating thought:

> When density, spatial mobility, ethnic and class hetero-geneity, and anonymity of the city are combined with poverty, physical deterioration, poor education, unemployment, and a wide range of other negative characteristics, it is logical to assume that urban life generates lawlessness and deviance, especially among its most deprived citizens. These assumptions have not been proven, but they support the belief that the cumulative effects of urban life produce violence and crime.[20]

The author confesses all of this to be unsupported assumptions. But they offer theoretical justification for his theory.

Are we also justified in imputing the fear of American cities to the other cities of the world? One of the classic virtues of the study of cultural anthropology is its reminder that cultural systems have great differences as well as similarities. One of the virtues of contemporary studies in urban anthropology is its reminder that we cannot judge the sins (or virtues) of the world's cities by extrapolating from the problems and issues we find on the streets of Chicago. Little research has yet been done of crime patterns in urban cultures outside North America and Europe. What has been done seems to affirm that "crime rates are higher in urban areas of the United States than in urban centers in other countries."[21] Which is the gnat, and which is the camel that we continue to swallow?

WHAT IS THE REAL PROBLEM?

We must search elsewhere to find the causes of our fear of the city. Our generalizations about crime have too many exceptions to remain valid generalizations. Where will we look? One part of the puzzle is the assumptions and values that are vested in the observers. White North Americans carry a lot of invisible baggage when they step onto the subway platform in the city.

1. *White ethnocentrism* continues to influence us. Non-English-speaking and/or "nonwhite" peoples have always been viewed with suspicion by whites in the New World. When labor shortages in the British homeland after 1718 began to induce that government to place restrictions on immigration, authorities opened the doors of the American Colonies to non-English nationalities for economic reasons. But the new immigrants met with open hostility. Benjamin Franklin wrote in 1751:

> Why should the Palatine boors be suffered to swarm into our settlements, and, by herding together, establish their language and manners, to the exclusion of ours? Why should Pennsylvania, founded by the English, become a colony of aliens, who will shortly be so numerous as to Germanize us, instead of our Anglifying them . . . ?[22]

The ideological picture of America as an asylum for all comers did not sway the founding fathers at the Constitutional Convention as they carried on protracted debates over whether to declare naturalized citizens ineligible for Congress. Nor did it affect the frontier dispossession of Native American lands, even into the twentieth century. Between 1887 and 1934, tribal holdings fell from 138 million acres to 56 million acres, "most of which has been judged by soil conservationists to be severely or critically eroded."[23]

As immigration patterns by the end of the nineteenth century began to draw more and more southern Europeans and Asians to the United States, ethnic attitudes intensified. The connection between immigration and crime became something of a national obsession. The United States Immigration Commission carried out a series of studies of the "immigration problem," devoting a whole volume to "Immigrants and Crime." It drew a composite picture of "races and nationalities . . . exhibiting clearly defined criminal characteristics."[24] Italians, Greeks, Irish, French, and Jews were associated with murder, prostitution, burglary, and larceny. The report did not attempt to explain the observed relationship between crime and ethnicity. Nor did it consider the possibility that the correlation was somehow related to poverty. Crime could be reduced by restricting the immigration of those "races" that were prone to criminality.

Today, of course, it is "blacks, Puerto Ricans, and Chicanos" who are blamed for high rates of crime. As always, crime is seen as an ethnic, cultural aberration. It is true that urban crime rates are much higher for blacks than whites, particularly in violent street crimes. But it is also true that blacks are more likely to be arrested on suspicion than whites. And it is true as well that blacks have low arrest rates for white-collar crimes such as tax evasion, embezzlement, and price fixing.

Although the majority of street crime is black against black, middle-class whites often see crime as a matter of black against white. Race, rather than crime, becomes the object of judgment in the city. There has been an ethnic judgment in all white perceptions of urban crime. In the 1860s it was the Irish and their "intemperate disposition." In the 1960s it was the blacks and their "disrespect for law." If beauty is in the eye of the beholder, crime is in the same beholder's perception of skin color and ethnicity.

How we see can be changed. Lee Holthaus serves as director of the Union Rescue Mission of Los Angeles. With an annual operating budget of $2.9 million, the hundred-year-old mission he superintends reaches out to drug addicts, alcoholics, unwed expectant mothers, homosexuals, and street transients. They come from every imaginable ethnic and language group. But they share one thing in common: there are no human support systems for them. How does Holthaus, after twenty years in the navy and service as an adviser to the White House in telecommunications, keep from discouragement and frustration in this ministry? He says,

> When I see a street person I must not see: a man with lice or mental illness; a man who may sell or destroy anything of value I may give him; a man who has spent years on a mission program and gained little of permanent value because he is back on the street; a man content to sit idly in our Chapel all day— day after day. Instead, I must see Jesus. If I see the man as Jesus, I am guarded against seeing him with contemptuous eyes.[25]

Where, Holthaus asks, do we see Jesus in the story of the Good Samaritan? Usually as the one who is willing to help the hated. But have we displaced Jesus? Does Jesus not picture Himself in this parable as the beaten and robbed man there on the road? It makes a difference how we see.

Looking at the Humboldt Park area of northwest Chicago can reinforce the fears we have discussed. Vacant buildings are defaced by gang graffiti. The Latin Kings, the Spanish Cobras—each gang marks out its turf on the walls. The neighborhood has one of the highest rates of youth violence in the city. Jobs are very hard to find, there is a 75 percent dropout rate from the schools, and drugs feed the anger of the community.

Yet in 1977 Manny Ortiz and his brothers and sisters in Christ saw something different in Humboldt Park. "We've given the community an alternative—the kingdom of God," Ortiz comments. The alternative vision has included a multi-ethnic church, Spirit and Truth Fellowship (now spinning off four congregations), a food pantry, a thrift shop, the Community Christian School with two hundred pupils, and a center offering family and legal counseling. "I saw the grace of God through these people," comments the church's youth director, a former heroin addict. "We claim the city for the Lord," says Ortiz. "We're here to occupy it until He comes."[26]

Several organizing principles were hammered out by the core

group of about seven families who began the ministry: How will we live out the gospel in our context? How will we develop indigenous leadership? How can we work out our discipleship and apprenticeship programs on the local level in an urban situation? How will our evangelism be incarnational and holistic? Among all these was one that speaks to the enclave mentality of ethnocentrism: "Since our community was not homogeneous, our church could not be."[27]

2. *Success* as a middle-class self-perception also plays an important part in how we see the city. In keeping with other American cultural assumptions, the push to self-achievement is usually measured in material terms or, if not, in visible ways. The achievement of physical comfort, good health and "decent" medical facilities, and an "adequate" standard of living become rules of thumb that draw for the "average American" a circle of success large enough for him or her to feel comfortable with and still keep pushing for more.[28]

How, then, do people who hold these values react when they see the city? It is not the crime that turns us from the city. It is dilapidated housing, gutters filled with trash and debris, graffiti on the walls of buildings and streetcars. They become symbols verbalizing failure and lack of achievement. The people of the city are defined in terms of the homeless, the shiftless, the welfare recipient. The poor are redefined from the economically marginalized to the "losers." People in the city are poor because they lack initiative, drive, and the other attributes needed in the push toward success. "Losers," in fact, are all that are seen in the city. The young, urban professionals ("Yuppies") or the hard-working blue-collar laborers become "invisible people," their presence minimized by the suburbanites' cultural aspirations oriented by success and expecting only failure in the city.

This same "success ideal" in the United States mythologizes the suburban way of life. "As society continues to equate success with location, the idealization of suburbia becomes a broad cultural value, exerting its pull on the city dweller and helping to empty previously acceptable urban areas."[29] Urban communities are devalued by a low-priority status. Park Avenue and Harlem become more than districts or street names in Manhattan; they become verbal symbols of success and failure.

In the meantime, the city's poor—no mean psychologists themselves—identify the presence of the church with those who are able to "make it." It becomes in some areas a powerful argument against the gospel itself. People outside the church describe themselves to visiting clergy as feeling "too bad to belong to it." Others find their faith strengthened and their commitment deepened by participating in a church prepared to deal with failure. The vicar of a small but lively congregation in Liverpool, England, says to his bishop, "I want to say something about new vicars; they've got to be able to live with failure." He continues, "People are pleased when I fail. I wouldn't say pleased exactly. But they experience failure so much. If I say that I've failed again, that reassures them. Sharing it reassures me too. We clergy don't have to be too anxious about people seeing our humanness."[30] The church that plans to succeed in the city must risk losing its image of success and respectability.

When the biblical picture of success as foot washing (John 13:5–7) and baptism by crucifixion (Mark 10:39–45) replaces the church's search for fifty-yard-line tickets in glory, we will have learned how to be Number One (Mark 10:44). Steve De Bernardi, founder-director of San Francisco's Harvest Ministry, suggests a concrete way to learn.

De Bernardi is "pastor" to the residents of some 225 San Francisco hotels. Not the Hiltons or the Holiday Inns, but those residential hotels where most pay $250 a month for one little room without a bathroom. His congregation are the elderly living on fixed incomes, the middle-aged down on their luck, retired merchant seamen who have nowhere else to go. The hotel becomes his parish, with a regular routine of Bible studies, visits to the hospital or health clinic, somebody who needs to go to

Social Security to sign up for food stamps. His biggest frustration? "Having a desire to see large numbers of people make drastic changes, and not seeing that happen. And it may never happen. . . . It's not a cost-productive kind of ministry." His greatest need? "People. We need people committed to working in the inner city and giving their time. That's the greatest need."

What needs to be done? There must be a parish concept that will encourage teams of Christians to adopt a hotel and begin to minister one-to-one or to a family. He pleads for individual churches to adopt a hotel and accept its residents into the church family. "This would mean bringing them to church, to picnics, and to family gatherings and dinners. It would involve having study with them. But most of all, just loving them. They will teach Christians a great deal about ministry if Christians give themselves to them. And churches will be blessed because of their interaction with the poor. That's God's promise."[31]

Youth With a Mission (YWAM) has been an urban foot-washer since its beginnings in 1971 in Kabul, Afghanistan. Frustrated by its traditional evangelistic approach to the American and European hippies traveling through the city, it changed its focus. What was needed, it found, was a caring Christian community that offered love and acceptance to alienated, wounded young people. In 1973 a team moved to Amsterdam, only 3 percent of whose population were churchgoers. Under the leadership of Floyd McClung, and after two years of prayer and planning, "Urban Missions" was finally launched. Evolving over the years into four live-in communities, the ministry now sends eighty staff members into a variety of places of service. These include coffee bars, street preaching, social work with prostitutes, drop-in centers, drama teams, an elementary school, literature distribution, home Bible studies, and concerts. McClung writes,

> On Friday and Saturday nights a small group goes out to witness to the prostitutes, who number as many as fifteen thousand in Amsterdam's inner city. This activity has led to many dramatic conversions. It also reminds us of people's

resistance to the gospel. Further, these experiences strengthen our conviction that the city is best penetrated by a praising, loving community that raises questions in people's minds by the love, creative evangelism, and practical care within the community.[32]

YWAM's definition of success is a slogan: "Take Amsterdam for Christ!"

3. Progress and optimism add still another dimension to white perceptions of the city. Almost a cult in the United States, the concept of progress is interrelated with material well-being and a general optimism toward the future. "Most Americans feel that through their efforts a better future can be brought about which will not compromise the welfare and progress of others. There is enough for everyone—a belief which is valid for people living in a country with an expanding economy and rich resources."[33]

Rooted originally in the Puritan hope that New England would one day become the New Jerusalem, the theological sense of Millennium was transposed into a secularized sense of the advance of mankind toward the future. By the end of the nineteenth century, the concept of progress had become almost as sacred to Americans of all classes as it had in its beginnings—but God had been replaced with an emphasis on industry and technology. "You can't stop progress" became a national colloquialism. The Chicago Fair of 1893 drew 27 million visitors confirming faith in progress. The aim of that exhibit, one visitor declared, was "to seize the living scroll of human progress, inscribed with every successive conquest of man's intellect."[34]

That confidence did not diminish with time. As late as 1933, at the very bottom of the Depression, Chicago staged another world's fair to celebrate "A Century of Progress." When Robert and Helen Lynd first visited Muncie, Indiana, in the 1920s for research on their anthropological classic, *Middletown,* they found faith in progress, now secularized, a religious article of commitment. And when they revisited Muncie during the Depression, to prepare *Middletown in Transition* (1937), they found that same confidence in progress largely undimmed.

As this concept confronted the rise of the American city, however, deep suspicions about the city began to grow. Nineteenth-century writers like Herman Melville, Nathaniel Hawthorne, and Edgar Allan Poe were disturbed and offended by the American city's effect on the human spirit in the period before the Civil War. For them the city scene became a "backdrop for frightening experiences, personal defeat, icy intellectualism, heartless commercialism, miserable poverty, crime and sin, smoke and noise, dusk and loneliness."[35] "All towns"—to repeat Hawthorne's grim advice—"should be made capable of purification by fire, or of decay, within each half-century." Henry Adams, the displaced patrician, commented on the San Francisco earthquake of 1906:

> San Francisco burned down last week, and I have been searching the reports to learn whether the whole city contained one object that cannot be replaced better in six months. As yet I've heard of nothing.

Progress meant freedom; it meant power. But the city meant imprisonment in artificiality, the loss of individualism. Increasingly, under the wearing impact of industrialization, it was seen as a malignant social system, a cancer or a tumor. John Dewey lamented the decline of neighborliness in the city. Robert Park, the father of American urban studies and a colleague of Dewey at the University of Chicago, shared Dewey's frustration.

With the growth of black and ethnic minority populations in the city, white hopes for progress and positive change grew less and less. The loss of a tax base through the departure of the white wage-earners, the consequent deterioration of housing, and urban race riots all served to multiply despair over the possibility of change.

In the meantime, these same perspectives of progress and optimism fed black anger and frustration. Hope had brought the black from the South to the northern cities. The black had bought the "American Dream," encouraged by voices like those of Booker T. Washington. Prophets like Malcolm X arose to remind them that "white is still right." And the desperation and anger over unfulfilled assumptions exploded on the streets of America's cities. Progress, the black still believed, meant freedom—but in the city some were more free than others. Progress still meant power—but not for a culture now learning to live with a self-image of hate imposed by white power brokers.

The city, for both black and white, had become a tomb not open to change or progress. Promise had become threat; change had become survival.

How do we change these perceptions of the city? We revolt against the definition of progress that feeds them. We take our towels and our crosses and discard our "let's make a deal" way of living. Progress for the Christian becomes, not a goal to be pursued, but "the unexpected surprise of a life lived in service."[36]

Like John Perkins, we carry our new dreams into northwest Pasadena, California. There, in a setting with one of the highest daytime crime rates in the state, where 35 percent of the community's teenagers are unemployed, we rebuild the city by rebuilding our memory of the old Puritan millennial center—Jesus Christ as the Lord of the city. The Harambee Discipleship House is born, providing a home environment where approximately ten young black men committed to Christ can be nurtured in their faith. The Harambee Christian Family Center opens its doors with a comprehensive and visionary ministry to rebuild the family. A summer outreach program for neighborhood children between the ages of four and fourteen mixes Bible study with arts and crafts, cooking, sewing, woodworking, reading, and bicycle repair. The Harambee Youth Force provides eighteen young people with summer employment. A school of business prepares to open its doors on Monday evenings. Skills development classes, individual tutoring, and Bible study hours are scheduled for students in grades one through twelve.[37]

And what motivates Perkins in all this? "My fondest dream for my country," he states, "is that God would raise up an army of Nehemiahs who could relocate in every community of need throughout the land, and live out the gospel that brings liberty and justice. God *can* heal our land!"[38]

4. Patterns of commitment also influence the way the city is seen. Americans are action oriented; they are "doers." Edward C. Stewart defines this quality:

> Action and hard work will bring about what the individual wants; hence, Americans are described as having the attribute of effort-optimism. Through one's effort or hard work one will achieve one's ambitions. No goal is too remote, no obstacle is too difficult, for the individual who has the will and the determination and who expends the effort. Hard work is rewarded by success.[39]

The city rises to frustrate this effort-optimism. Competing street values, the lack of hope amid affluence, urban social programs whose "trickle down" intentions never trickle down to the street, underemployment, hunger, poor schools—all combine to cry out failure. The Americans, with a commitment fenced around by a success motivation oriented to progress and the future, look for other answers. Failure, they decide, means the individual did not try hard enough, is lazy or worthless. Achievement has to be visible and measurable.

Deprived of that visible success, the Americans find the city difficult to handle. Finally they confront the situation with a "let's get the heck out of here" attitude. Their sights are shifted toward a different future achievement, or they disregard the present problems as the fault of the people in the city who have created them. They come to the city with the proverbial wisdom, "Where there's a will, there's a way." And the city shrugs its shoulders.

Our vision for the city has been dimmed by cultural expectations that affect even a Christian perspective. Our patterns of commitment have been shaped by a telescopic idealism too easily defeated by urban realities. Biblical commitment begins with other kinds of questions: What are God's intentions for the human future in the city? How may we be co-laborers with God in bringing forth a new age of righteousness, justice, peace, and reconciliation?

Tom Sine suggests,

> We can directly derive our sense of biblical mission today from the intentions of God for tomorrow. He intends nothing less than the total redemption of his people and his world. And if that's what he is up to, then we need to again become a people of courageous visions and transcendent dreams.[40]

The work of the Spirit is to bring into being the urban vision of the Lord. At Pentecost the Lord empowers with a vision of *shalom*. The Old Testament promised that God would create a people who will see and serve the future of God. Pentecost becomes the beginning of that Old Testament hope.

That vision is the compelling center of the Lord's Prayer. The first three petitions of it ("Hallowed be thy name, Thy kingdom come, Thy will be done, on earth as it is in heaven") "are actually three ways of expressing the same urgent petition: the redemption of God's fallen and rebellious creation."[41] In praying for the coming of that kingdom we pray for a redeemed, healed, and transformed city. The prayer is future oriented, the "not yet" of longing and hope for the day of consummation brought by God alone. And yet it is also oriented to the "now," the "already"; we are asking God to begin now what He will complete at the Last Day.

David Bosch says of the Lord's Prayer,

> To offer that prayer implies believing Christians make a difference to this world, that things are not to remain the way they are. It implies having a vision of a new society and working for it as though it is attainable. It means in other words, getting involved in God's mission in the world, and calling people to faith in Christ [in order to] share in the mission of transforming the world.[42]

Our culturally shaped patterns of commitment work against this calling to service and prayer in the city. We become content with little dreams and limited expectations. Because we "know" that not all will accept the gospel in the city, that not all evil, injustice, and exploitation will be corrected, we become satisfied with retrenchment, escape, and failure. We are afraid to aim at God's stars, and we detach ourselves from depth of involvement.

But everywhere there are those who are kingdom advocates in the city. In Caracas, Venezuela, Godofredo Marín promotes a new evangelical political party, ORA. The acronym literally means "pray" in Spanish and stands for Authentic Renewal Organization. Marín is building grass-roots support before the party puts forward candidates for major political posts. He finds Catholics as well as Protestants interested in ORA. There are no requirements that supporters must become evangelicals to belong to the party, but they must subscribe to its guiding principles. These Marín has drawn from the Protestant Reformation. "The only faith that produces social development is faith in Christ," the chemical engineering professor tells groups, secular or Christian.

In Buenos Aires, Carlos Gattinoni, the bishop emeritus of the Methodist Church, serves on a ten-man presidential commission charged with finding, or accounting for, the thousands killed or missing in the governmental rampage of the 1970s. He has written nearly all the evangelistic flyers and booklets in use by the church. His concern for people has led him also into the struggle for human rights.

Gattinoni said few evangelical leaders spoke out against the military's ruthless suppression of dissent in the seventies. Either churches didn't know what was happening, or "it was so horrible we didn't want to recognize it." Now he often finds himself with grief-stricken parents or friends of the missing. "I tell them, 'Reach out and grab onto God, and open your heart to Jesus.' Sometimes they break out crying. . . . For these problems there's no other solution than Jesus Christ."[43]

What advice does the bishop give us about fear in the city?

First, we must not forget that the center of everything is personal redemption in Christ. Second, the absolute Lordship of Christ in every aspect of one's life is essential. Third, we must not mutilate the gospel by teaching only the joy of Christianity and not also the cross.[44]

A good antidote to fear in any city.

NOTES

[1] J. John Palen, *The Urban World* (New York: McGraw-Hill, 1981), p. 267.

[2] Quoted in James Spates and John J. Macionis, *The Sociology of Cities* (New York: St. Martin's, 1982), pp. 430–31.

[3] Alan S. Berger, *The City: Urban Communities and Their Problems* (Dubuque, Ia.: William C. Brown, 1978), p. 413.

[4] Palen, *The Urban World,* pp. 267–68.

[5] Morton White and Lucia White, *The Intellectual Versus the City* (New York: Oxford University Press, 1977), pp. 194–95.

[6] John Maust, *Cities of Change: Urban Growth and God's People in Ten Latin American Cities* (Coral Gables, Fla.: Latin America Mission, 1984), p. 21.

[7] Ibid., p. 127.

[8] Roger S. Greenway, "Let These Women Go! Prostitution and the Church," *Urban Mission* 1, no. 4 (March 1984): 17.

[9] Edward R. Dayton and Samuel Wilson, eds., *Unreached Peoples '82* (Elgin, Ill.: David C. Cook, 1982), p. 141.

[10] Esther Arias and Mortimer Arias, *The Cry of My People* (New York: Friendship, 1980), pp. 70–71.

[11] James Goff and Margaret Goff, *In Every Person Who Hopes . . .* (New York: Friendship, 1980), p. 46.

[12] Josef Gugler and William G. Flanagan, *Urbanization and Social Change in West Africa* (New York: Cambridge University Press, 1978), p. 42.

[13] For a detailed picture of this process, consult William J. Hanna and Judith L. Hanna, *Urban Dynamics in Black Africa* (New York: Aldine, 1981), pp. 175–93.

[14] P'Bitek Okot, *Song of Lawino* (Nairobi: East African Publishing House, 1966), pp. 188–89.

[15] Mark Abrahamson, *Urban Sociology* (Englewood Cliffs, N.J.: Prentice-Hall, 1980), p. 291.

[16] Barry Schwartz, ed., *The Changing Face of the Suburbs* (Chicago: University of Chicago Press, 1976), p. 155.

[17] Palen, *The Urban World,* p. 269.

[18] John W. Bardo and John J. Hartman, *Urban Sociology* (Wichita, Kans.: Wichita State University, 1982), p. 235.

[19] Wendell H. Oswalt, *Understanding Our Culture: An Anthropological View* (New York: Holt, Rinehart and Winston, 1970), pp. 121, 127.

[20] Berger, *The City,* p. 414.

[21] Bardo and Hartman, *Urban Sociology,* p. 234.

[22] Quoted in Stephen Steinberg, *The Ethnic Myth* (New York: Atheneum, 1981), p. 11.

[23] *New York Times Magazine* (11 February 1979): 32.

[24] "Immigrants and Crime," *United States Immigration Commission,* vol. 36 (Washington: Government Printing Office, 1911), p. 2.

[25] Lee Holthaus, "Changing Lives Since 1891: The Union Rescue Mission of Los Angeles," *Urban Mission* 2, no. 2 (November 1984): 14.

[26] "Claiming Turf in Hispanic Chicago," *Eternity* 35, no. 6 (June 1984): 25.

[27] Manuel Ortiz, "A Church in Missiological Tension," *Urban Mission* 2, no. 1 (September 1984): 13.

[28] Edward C. Stewart, *American Cultural Patterns: A Cross-Cultural Perspective* (LaGrange Park, Ill.: Intercultural Network, 1972), pp. 39–42.

[29] Walter E. Ziegenhals, *Urban Churches in Transition* (New York: Pilgrim, 1978), p. 60.

[30] David Sheppard, *Bias to the Poor* (London: Hodder and Stoughton, 1983), p. 47.

[31] "Making the Hotel My Parish," *Bridges* 1, no. 2 (Fall 1984): 5.

[32] Floyd McClung, "Urban Missions: Reaching the City of Amsterdam," in Dayton and Wilson, *Unreached Peoples '82,* p. 63.

[33] Stewart, *American Cultural Patterns,* p. 66.

[34] Robert Nisbet, *History of the Idea of Progress* (New York: Basic, 1980), p. 204.

[35] White and White, *The Intellectual Versus the City,* p. 37.

[36] Tom Sine, *The Mustard Seed Conspiracy* (Waco, Tex.: Word, 1981), p. 78.

[37] Bill Sherwood, "Revitalizing Northwest Pasadena," *Bridges* 1, no. 2 (Fall 1984): 10–11.

[38] John Perkins, *With Justice for All* (Ventura, Calif.: Regal, 1982), p. 197.

[39] Stewart, *American Cultural Patterns,* p. 38.

[40] Sine, *The Mustard Seed Conspiracy,* p. 185.

[41] Quoted in Mortimer Arias, *Announcing the Reign of God* (Philadelphia: Fortress, 1984), p. 31.

[42] David Bosch, *Witness to the World* (London: Marshall, Morgan and Scott, 1980), p. 244.

[43] Maust, *Cities of Change,* p. 102.

[44] Ibid.

Chapter Four

The Secularization Myth:
"Any Faith Dies in the City"

The Secularization Myth: "Any Faith Dies in the City"

Harvey Cox said it in the 1960s: "The rise of urban civilization and the collapse of traditional religion are the two main hallmarks of our era and are closely related movements."[1] Our urban world, he wrote, is not persecuting religion; it simply bypasses and undercuts it, going on to other things. The age of the secular city is an age of "no religion at all." Religion still remains for some a hobby, for others a mark of national or ethnic identity, for still others an aesthetic delight. We may study it, invoke it at presidential inaugurations, and enjoy the buildings in which fewer and fewer practice it. But for most it no longer provides "an inclusive and commanding system of personal and cosmic values and explanation."[2] Humanity is supposed to have come of age in the city, but religion is no longer part of that growing-up process.

A graduate of the University of Tanzania underlines the argument. "Where I come from, religion is a natural part of life. But here, in the urban areas, everything is a hodgepodge. Family and traditional ties are broken, and other influences take over. The church suffers." Timothy Monsma adds, "Secularism is growing rapidly in Africa and those who benefit from upward mobility seem the most vulnerable."[3]

Education, literature, and entertainment are said to draw people away from urban Africa's traditional union of the sacred and the secular. Even the church is touched. F. V. Tate writes of Nairobi, Kenya, "The majority of those with some Christian background cease to associate with the organized church in town."[4] One scholar speaks of at least 200,000 inactive Protestant migrants in Kinshasa, Zaire, compared with 31,000 active members. The frustration boils over in the language of one Catholic author: "The church is simply not organized to deal with the urban scene."

Sheep tend to stray in the city. In the cities we find the fastest growth, the largest churches. And here also we agonize over the most rapid decline and the easiest nominalism. Is it true, as Benjamin Tonna suggests, that "urbanization and secularization go hand in hand as parallel processes"?[5]

North America has always had its prophets to answer yes to that question. In 1816 the Female Missionary Society launched religious work among the poor of New York; its appointed missionary, Ward Stafford, saw the city's poor wards as "a great mass of people beyond the restraints of religion." By 1862, a Congregationalist leader was warning that 60 percent of New York's population was unreached by Protestant churches and that things were just as bad in other cities. Josiah Strong's book *Our Country* (1885) repeated the charges. Chicago, Strong said, had seen its church population plummet from one for every 747 persons in 1840 to one for every 2,080 in 1880; in many big cities, vast districts were utterly destitute of the gospel.

At that time, people were writing books with titles like *Modern Cities and Their Religious Problems* (1887). And something called "the Charity Organization Movement" was formed to seek to build character and moral uplift among the urban poor. Jane Addams began her Hull House in Chicago (1889). Josephine

Lowell helped to found the New York City Charity Organization Society (1882). The list was long, the needs seen as massive.[6]

Behind much of this strategy was the assumption we have dealt with before in this study, the assumed conflict between life in the city and life in the village. A book by John Lancaster Spalding in 1880 drew the polarization sharply. The farmer, argued this parish priest in New York, is "the strongest and the healthiest member of the social body; he is also the most religious and the most moral." With greater moral purity and a deep commitment that it is good to believe in God and the soul, the farmer's life "more than the city conduces to happiness and morality and . . . harmonizes better with the Christian ideal."[7] And by contrast, he continues, there is the city. It draws to itself "those who desire to lead a life of dissipation." In the city you see "moral degradation," "the grossest sensuality," family life destroyed, and "ancestral traditions . . . not so much forgotten as buried." The dismal list is endless. His conclusion?

> It is far from my thought to say that the city is wholly evil. . . .
> But if those I love were rich I should not wish them to live in
> the city; and if they were poor, and made it their dwelling-
> place, I should despair of them.[8]

There were some who wondered whether revivals would work in an urban setting. Early nineteenth-century revivalists had already noticed their success was greater in small towns than in cities. Even Charles Finney, the father of modern revivalism, expressed concern over city people too engrossed in worldly ambitions.

> See how crazy these are who are scrambling to get up, . . .
> enlarging their houses, changing their styles of living. . . . It is
> like climbing up [the] masthead to be thrown off into the ocean.
> To enjoy God you must come down, not go up there.[9]

Time has not fully swept away that mentality. In 1962 Truman B. Douglass referred to a study in which a sampling of 1,709 ministerial students found that only 36 percent came from cities of more than 250,000 population. "Because of their rural and small-town origins," he argued, "many ministers bring to their work in a city church a distaste for city ways—a distaste which is the more disabling because it is largely unconscious."[10] The piety patterns of the rural church see the city as a secular menace.

CONFLICTING INFORMATION

But is all this true? Is secularization one of the "basic dimensions of urbanism," an urban part of "the fundamental difference between ruralism and urbanism"?[11]

Even Harvey Cox has had to backtrack a bit. Almost twenty years after unfolding his vision of the modern technological city and its secular style, he has looked again.[12] Religion seems alive and fresh in the secular city. The populist piety of fundamentalism and Jerry Falwell and the uninvited voice of liberation theology are said to have arisen from the ashes to challenge our postmodern world. They are reminders that

> we need a *postmodern* theology in order to cope not with the decline of religion but with its resurgence; not with the death of God but with the rebirth of gods; not with spreading skepticism but with a new sense of the sacred; not with private piety but with political faith.[13]

Religion may indeed be returning to the secular city. But Cox insists, "No one can move beyond the secular city who has not first passed through it."[14]

The cities of the Third World, according to Tonna, seem not to have

> been administered such a massive dose of secularization. Those in Latin America are permeated by a popular religiosity with Christian tinting. The cities of Africa reflect the influence of traditional religions—Islamic and Christian—although the distinction between religion and religious institution has begun to make its presence felt. The cities of Asia have their own religious coloring (excluding perhaps Japan and Hong Kong);

even Saigon and Hanoi allow Christian religious institutions to maintain a viable presence.[15]

The resurgence of the Christian church in the Peoples Republic of China reminds us that faith dies hard. In spite of the Red Guard and the Cultural Revolution, in spite of a massive educational campaign launched by Maoist secularization, religious institutions refuse to stay buried in China's cities.

Massive migration patterns into the cities do not dissipate religious commitments on the road from the village to the metropolis. In Lagos, Nigeria, religious groups are among the first organizations sought out by migrants after they arrive in the city. While they ordinarily wait several years to join other types of voluntary associations, they usually find their religious groups within the first year.[16]

Migration patterns from the Third World to the United States show this same stability and commitment to the traditional faith of the homeland. The south end of Dearborn, Michigan, a suburb of Detroit, is a community of approximately five thousand people, of which more than half are of Arab-Muslim cultural descent. The majority in this low-to-middle income, working-class community are immigrants, and two-thirds have lived in this area five years or more. It is probably the largest Muslim community in the United States.

Has the city secularized this people's commitment to Islam? A doctoral dissertation issued in 1964 emphasizes the contrary. Their faith has acted as a basis for the unity of the community. The traditional groupings of Islam, both the Sunni and Shia sects, retain their integrity and separate identities even in the new setting. Separate mosques, sectarian rituals, and different burial sites are maintained. In the meantime, shifts in marriage and family patterns show clear signs of American acculturation. But religious adjustments are few.[17]

In fact, this pattern is not out of keeping with Muslim traditions in the Middle East. The city has often possessed a special sanctity for the Muslim community. Cities "are regarded as the sole places in which a full and truly Muslim life may be lived."[18] Urban-rural divisions were exceptions to the Muslim rule of religio-communal bonds between town dwellers and the peoples of the hinterland. Given that bond, "nothing . . . leads us to believe that Middle Eastern villagers and city dwellers differ essentially in the religious aspect of life."[19]

European migration patterns from Christian communities to the United States yield similar results. Czechs, Poles, Germans, Jews, and Irish gathered together in cultural neighborhoods in the New World. There they shaped the urban villages we call "ghettos" in the industrial centers of North America. There they carried on Old World social, familial, and religious customs.

> Carrying their beliefs with them to America, the immigrants attempted to recreate their communal life of the Old World by implanting their traditional religion in America. . . . Religion was intertwined and imbedded in the psyche, the folklife, the very identity of each immigrant. It gave meaning, a system of moral values, self-definition, and community to the immigrants. It ordered their internal, private world and the world outside the family. Thrown into close proximity with competing cultural and linguistic groups in urban, industrial America, the immigrants turned to religion, the very bone and sinew of ethnicity, to shore up communal ties. With family and job, religion was the focal point of immigrant life.[20]

What is the overall shape of church life in the central cities of the United States? How does it compare with rural America? Russell Hale spent a year studying and interviewing people in selected counties of the nation with exceptionally high rates of alienation from established churches. From this research came his book *The Unchurched: Who They Are and Why They Stay Away.* Hale says his

> findings would suggest that, contrary to popular opinion, the unchurched phenomenon in the United States may be primarily rural rather than urban. Such an hypothesis needs

further testing. Provisionally, however, one is impressed that ten of the fifteen largest cities in the United States have unchurched rates well *below* the national average.[21]

Using less scientifically obtained data, Charles Chaney concurs, at least with respect to the evangelical community. Evangelical Christianity, he argues, does not reside mostly in the suburbs.

> Actually, suburbs, with only 16 percent of the evangelicals and 27 percent of the populace, are less evangelical than the nonmetropolitan cities, small towns, rural areas and *inner cities* of this nation. The central cities of America, alleged by many to be barren deserts as far as evangelical Christianity is concerned, have about one-third of the nation's total population. They also have one-third of America's evangelicals.[22]

What accounts for this strong evangelical presence in the central cities? The tremendous achievement in evangelism and church planting carried on by black churches and their leaders throughout this century. In 1899, only five black churches were reported in Chicago, although the black population was near 30,000. By 1940, one very conservative count placed 250 black churches in that city with more than 135,000 members. By 1982, Chaney estimates, there were close to 1,750 black Baptist churches alone, with 350,000 members. He adds,

> Multiply this kind of pattern by all the American cities where there are large black communities—especially black communities that have developed since 1945—and you'll have a picture of the accomplishment in church planting that has taken place.[23]

It is a black community, as well, that has not locked up its faith behind church doors. The black "Bible-believing" community, unlike its white evangelical counterpart, has not suffered a radical break between a life of faith and its exhibition in urban society and politics. The civil rights movement of the 1960s was fed by churches on their knees in prayer in the streets of Selma and Birmingham. Passivity in the face of urban secularization cannot be charged to Martin Luther King, Jr., or to Jesse Jackson. The black preacher has swayed churches in Watts and delegates at Democratic National Conventions.

The largest congregation in Philadelphia, Deliverance Evangelistic Church, has more than forty separate evangelistic ministries. This church purchased a large piece of property in an area regarded by some as one of the most economically deprived neighborhoods of the city. In July 1985 the congregation broke ground for the first of a collection of buildings—not a church, but a twenty-one-store shopping center. Eventually there will be a hospital for the poor, a day-care center, and a school for the neighborhood. As a last step, the church building will be relocated there. Would Harvey Cox be willing to concede all this flows from "an inclusive and commanding system of personal and cosmic values and explanations"?

All this is certainly enough to question the adequacy of a term such as "suburbanization"—a concentration in the suburbs—to describe American religion. Though a full study of religion in suburban life remains unwritten, enough information is available to call into question past generalizations. Some studies of church attendance indicate rates are higher among urban residents than suburban. A 1968 study argues that

> the suburban return to religion resulted from the very forces that produced the suburban migration itself. In the case of religion, the postwar "baby boom," coupled with the traditional desire of American parents to provide a religious education for their children, was the outstanding factor. As the number of school-aged children in the general population declined so did the alleged religious revival.[24]

Suburban Americans are no more prone to religiosity than their urban counterparts. People still bring to the suburbs the spiritual furniture of their previous residence. It has been rearranged, some of it reupholstered. But a chair is still a chair, not a sofa.

PERCEPTIONS AND MISPERCEPTIONS

Before us now are two apparently contradictory perceptions: secularism as the basic reality of urban life, and religion as alive and well in the city. One scholar points to the influences of secularism and materialism in Africa now affecting the urban church even as much as ancestral cults and polygyny. Another points to Monrovia, Liberia, home of St. Peter's Lutheran Church—which had 120 persons baptized in the first few months of 1970—and the rapid growth of the church in Africa taking place in both the rural and the urban areas. One sees secularization as freeing city dwellers from traditional ties and making them open to the challenge of the gospel. Another sees secularization as reinforcing the old ties and leaving the urban centers still unmoved by the challenge of a new word about Jesus Christ.

Where does the truth lie? Probably somewhere in between: the city as both religious and secular, turning away from God and turning to Him as well. The secularist thesis needs many qualifications: (1) Secularism touches rural life as well as urban, suburban, and inner-city; (2) migration from a rural to an urban setting does not inevitably lead to a loss of faith; (3) sometimes faith becomes stronger under urban pressures, more essential in preserving the links with home and kin; (4) some faith systems (like Islam) are more resistant than others to alleged urban corrosion; (5) not all cities in all cultures show the same degree of secularism; (6) secularism may not always be the strongest reason for what some see to be the failure of the church in the city.

In the same spirit, the religious revival thesis also needs qualification: (1) Planting churches in the city is no simplistic guarantee of the conquest of secularism; (2) secularization can have a positive effect for church growth in addition to its negative impact; (3) secularism may make itself at home in the inner regions of a faith's world view long before it shows in external rituals and institutions; (4) the contemporary worldwide spread of Western lifestyle and technology is often the seedbed of secularism as well as an instrument in the propagation of the gospel.

101

Secularism, we are saying, is not exclusively an urban phenomenon, but it is certainly a real one. It has a deteriorating effect on faith, sometimes mortal to earnestly held convictions, Christian and otherwise. At the same time, its strength and flexibility can be overemphasized by those already timid toward the city. Misperceptions can accelerate alarm and exaggerate the dangers. Outlining the source of some of these mistaken generalizations can be helpful in keeping perspective. This can keep us from mythologizing the reality of secularism into the fiction of overwhelming secularization.

1. Recognizing that secularization may be mythologized is the first step in making progress toward understanding. Myths, we argue, are not simply fairy stories created by unthinking "primitives" to explain why lightning strikes or people dream. They are social fictions, created by the human heart out of its struggle with God, to represent what we want reality to be, not reflect what it is. Myths ideologize reality, using collected pieces of truth and bits of information—secularism in the city, for example—and out of this shape an illusion, something that will evoke vague and generalized images. And perhaps something that will help us flee God-given responsibility.

Contemporary myths spun in the West stem from science. Scientific conceptions are used to provide a tidy, simple, and all-purpose picture of the world.[25] Is this what Harvey Cox has done with secularization in the city? He has articulated a social fiction already widely held, a scientific myth of secularist images. So when one reads Harvey Cox, the city he pictures so eloquently seems less a place of flesh and stone than an image of something else. Even secularization has lost its negative edge under his handling. It seems interrelated, if not identical, with the kingdom of God. Is he talking about the cities we're talking about, or is he ideologizing an illusion about modern civilization? Is he talking about secularization in any negative sense, or is he ideologizing an illusion about human potential and progress?

Do those who fear the loss of faith in the city do the same thing from a reverse direction? For Cox the city becomes a positive image of progress and secularizing change. For evangelicals it becomes the epitome of loss and corruption. But for both it is an illusion that motivates—Cox toward the city, us away from it. In pharisaic concern over cups and pitchers tainted by city use, we perceive the city as the source of our outside pollution and forget that "whatever goes into the man from outside cannot defile him" (Mark 7:18). Worldliness is mythologized out of the human heart into a geographical area of great population density and heterogeneity. The Genesis history of Sodom is mythologized into an escape-from-the city theology. But we forget that Lot's problem was not his making peace with the city; it was his making peace with the violence, materialism, and sin of the city. That was present long before he went to dwell in Sodom. It was present in the country when he coveted the well-watered land that belonged to Abraham (Gen. 13:5–13); he could not see the wickedness for the water.

2. A deep part of the mythmaking comes from *the way we view religion*. Peter Glasner illustrates the various models created by the science of sociology to define the secularization process of human religions. The models are ideologized by science into social myths. And the myths, he continues, "are based on the acceptance of reified categories produced outside sociological analysis without recognizing them as such."[26] So, for example, there is preoccupation in much Western sociology with the institutionalized aspects of "religiosity." The assumption here is that a usable definition of Christianity must focus on function and be concerned with membership, ritual, and attendance. These become crucial elements of a definition of religion; so any move away from this institutional participation involves religious decline and secularism.

Has Africa become secularized on this basis? One counts the number of lapsed Christians and says yes. Or one counts the number of growing churches and says no.

103

If we are to break with this way of evaluating, we will have to see religion in a more sweeping, more holistic way. Can we do it by saying that human life, in its entirety, is religion, humanity's integral response action to God? Because it is totalitarian in its scope in that God's demands are all-embracing (Deut. 10:12–13; 2 Cor. 10:5), its progress or decline cannot be measured merely by church buildings or a lack of them; its measuring stick becomes its commitment to the words of the Preacher: "Fear God and keep His commandments, for this is the whole duty of man" (Eccl. 12:13).[27]

Viewed this way, secularization becomes a problem older than modernity that cannot easily be identified with the style of the modern technological city only.[28] It manifests itself wherever the human heart struggles to break free from the rule of God.

3. Identifying secularization with the city is an easy myth for North Americans to create. Generally we see ourselves sharply distinct from nature and from other forms of life. Guided by our stress on material things, we define nature's significance in terms of what can be harnessed for producing material welfare. Belief in the evil of human nature, even if an occasional American professes it, is overshadowed by the view of our ability to change our environment and be affected by it.[29] When we are sick, there is aspirin. When we are impoverished, there is work to get us what we need. The world and its cities are things we can control and use for self-improvement. The roots of secularism are all here.

How then does the myth of secularism develop? When we manipulate it from self-awareness before God into self-justification as "man come of age" in the city, when it becomes an "ideology of progress." Myths are self-defense mechanisms, not self-perception mirrors. Myths keep us from blaming ourselves as the guilty; they seek to fix responsibility elsewhere. Who can we blame? There is always the city. Blame the city for depersonalization, anarchy, anonymity, crime. Thus secularization as myth is understood, not as the enemy of the gospel, but its fruit.

4. The reality becomes the myth when *the church is not there to question the fusion*. And all too frequently that has been the case. The picture is frequently the same in Africa and Asia. Peter Falk writes that churches "have failed to realize fully the tremendous needs of the multitudes who left their homes and went to the cities. Not infrequently, Christians have moved to the cities before the church did so."[30] Has secularism created resistant cities? Or has church apathy fostered neglected cities? Are the unresponsive urbanites resistant, or neglected?

LESSONS TO BE LEARNED

Secularism is as present in the cities as it is in the country or the suburbs, and it has a corroding impact we cannot minimize. How should we respond to it?

1. Target the cities, do not flee them. Here are some of the church's greatest challenges. Waldron Scott, former general secretary of the World Evangelical Fellowship, tells of striking up a conversation with a young student in Bangkok.

> During our conversation I asked him, "Have you heard of Jesus Christ?"
> He responded, "Is that a new brand of soap?"
> At first I wanted to chuckle. Then I realized the enormity of what I had just heard: fully half of the world's people today—and quite possibly as many as two-thirds—do not know the difference between Jesus Christ and a bar of soap! Yet Dr. George Peters, a well-traveled observer, says, "I find very few of the mission societies who are really specializing in city evangelism."[31]

The question is not, will the church lose the city? The question is, will the church ever enter the city?

Everywhere the picture seems to be the same: not too many people or too much secularism, but too few churches. Bangkok boasts a population of 5.5 million, with Protestants and Catholics numbering at most 45,000, but only 102 churches as of 1983. Colombo, the capital of Sri Lanka, is the home of more than 600,000 people from eight different ethnic groups; only 51 local congregations exist to meet the needs of this city of fourteen square miles. The Soho district of London has a resident population of 3,000 to 4,000, with a working population of between 70,000 to 80,000 people. But church life in Soho, according to Michael Toogood,

> is practically non-existent. Two Roman Catholic churches are maintained largely by tourists and those who work in the area. The many Catholic residents are mainly nominal. The Anglican parish church was bombed in 1942 and has yet to be restored for use. A French Protestant church stands in the local square and attracts a small number of French-speaking people. The area has an active Hare Krishna group and an inactive Islamic center. There has been no resident evangelical witness in Soho for at least 100 years![32]

The problem in Soho is not primarily the dominance of secularism. It is the absence of the church and a Christian response to the need.

Charles Chaney suggests that the problem is the same in the United States. He divides America's population into three groups—the Insiders (sincere, ardent believers in Christ), the Sometimers (nominal Christians whose commitment never seriously affects the way they think or act), and the Outsiders (those who make no profession of faith in Christ at all). The vast majority of the Outsiders and Sometimers, he argues, are living in the great cities of our land. But "these are the very places where we have the fewest number of churches, proportionately."[33] Spotlighting the Southern Baptist commitment to the city, Chaney notes that 35.4 percent of the American population lives in the twenty-five largest Standard Metropolitan Statistical Areas (SMSAs), but only 8.7 percent of the existing Southern Baptist churches are located there. Less than 9 percent of the Southern Baptist Convention's churches are responsible for evangelizing 36 percent of the population.

2. Create a taxonomy of urban secularism. In looking at opposing generalizations and misperceptions we should see at least one thing clearly: Secularism and secularization at this point are categories more sermonic than scientific. The need of the hour is for us to make a careful and Christian examination of what makes secularism tick—specifically, what makes it tick in the city. Until that study is undertaken, little positive good will come from discussing secularization.

What sorts of questions need to be answered in this kind of research? Here are some from my growing list.

A. Does secularization need a more precise definition than the one we have suggested in this chapter? How can we develop a more precise definition and still retain an understanding of religion that cannot lose the biblical sense of wholeness we have argued for?

Empirical scholarship in the past has offered at least five different meanings of the term "secularization."[34] The first two we mention are the most problematic. First, secularization may be defined as "the decline of religion." On this basis, previously accepted doctrines, institutions, and symbols lose their influence and we end up with a religionless society and cities emptied of faith. But how does one measure such a decline? Given the nature of man and woman as the image of God, can we say that religion ever disappears?

Religion's direction may be displaced, turning from the Creator to the creation (Rom. 1:18–23), from the Overlord of the city to the city. But it does not disappear. So in Rio de Janeiro there is a high correlation of industrialization and growth of the Protestant church. "Similarly," according to C. W. Gates,

> most of the practicing Catholics are found in the urban areas. The 1950 census registered 93.5 percent of the Brazilian population as Roman Catholics. However, not more than 10 percent are in attendance at mass on a given Sunday. The large percentage of non-practicing Catholics are probably found

among the peasantry. It is in this extensive mass of the population that "folk-Catholicism" is found.[35]

Second, secularization may be viewed as "conformity with this world." In this case, attention is said to turn from the supernatural toward an exclusive concern with "this world." The end-result of this process is that the pragmatic tasks of the present become paramount and religion ceases to have any distinguishing identity. Again, how do we measure this kind of decay? And how does this model explain the capacity of religion to hang on in society? The model underlines the degenerative effects of secularization; it does not explain equally well the positive effects of secularization or the growth of religion in the so-called secular city. It assumes that "conformity with this world" is a negative effect. "Who is to say that concern for this world is not the authentic culmination of faith?"[36] Commitment to world change is certainly an essential feature of Christianity.

The three remaining models of secularization seem the most helpful and, in fact, may be complementary. They may be symbolized by the words "disengagement," "transposition," and "disenchantment."

Thus, as the third model we speak of the "disengagement of society from religion," society increasingly distancing itself from religion in such spheres as politics, education, and welfare. Religion is relegated to the private domain, with little or no effect on public life. "Transposition," the fourth model, represents a more radical shift. In it, counter-religious ideologies such as Marxism create a secular substitute, a revolutionary parallel to Christian eschatology. In North America, transposition creates civil religion, a political model embroidered with Christian terminology but leaving us with a radically altered design.

In cities and societies where disengagement is strong, one can expect the church and the Christian faith to be growing but compartmentalized into a narrow "religious" sphere where its vision for society is increasingly limited. In such a setting, the gospel will be squeezed into a narrowing channel of ecclesiocen-trism. The wider dimensions of the kingdom of God and its demands for all of life will lose the elbow room of the Spirit.

But in cities dominated by transpositional mentality, the difficulties will be even more restrictive. Pyongyang, once called the "Jerusalem of Korea," is now under a severely Marxist system and has not a single congregation openly meeting for worship. One expects society to be more restrictive in Peking the capital than in Canton the port city.

The fifth model of secularization is "disenchantment," the gradual loss of "a sense of the sacred" (Mircea Eliade). It is associated by scholars like Max Weber with the growth of a calculating rationality; it is said to be concerned for the best means rather than the best ends. Its results are seen in the corrosion of old beliefs and morality as the very basis of urban society.

> Who now needs a religious legitimation of the power of the state, when democracy is the order of the day? And who needs personal morality when "electronic eyes and data-retrieval systems have largely supplanted interpersonal concern and the deeply implanted virtues of honesty, industry, goodwill, responsibility and so on"?[37]

Urban society, under the impact of desacralization, becomes an iron cage, religion no longer socially significant in a deep way. It means, says Weber, the passing of a society in which the salt of the earth is still able to "sustain the social order."

But disenchantment as a model needs radical modifying. It assumes that such a desacralized society is virtually irretrievable, with little hope of revival. Like Weber, one is compelled to view the secular city with wistfulness for "the good old days" when the human city was not besieged by rationalization. In this thesis, modernity is perceived as closely linked to secularization. Weber traces the beginning of the end to the Protestant ethic of the sixteenth century and its connections with capitalism.

Is it this same nostalgia for a religious past that dominates our evangelical fear in losing our faith in the city? Even the fine writing of a Francis Schaeffer continually looks with dread on the effects of the loss of the rational process in human society. Do our contemporary examination of America's "Christian roots" and our deploring of its alleged loss operate from this same mythologizing of the golden past? In time past, were people more religious? Did modernity systematically disintegrate religion?

Anthropologist Mary Douglas berates this mythologizing of the past and rebukes those students of religion for having their eyes "glued to those conditions of modern life identified by Max Weber as antipathetic to religion."[38] Among other things, it assumes that moderns are utterly different from everyone else because of modernization and urbanization. This, she contends, is a case of tribal myopia. Have science, technology, and bureaucracy, she asks, really "quenched the sources of religious feeling and undermined religious authority"? The marvels of the modern urban society are at least as awesome as discoveries of a previous era. And the "vast impersonal bureaucratic machine" may indeed provoke crises of identity. But are not such as these the very stuff of the quest of faith since time immemorial? Further, have not the data we have mentioned in this chapter indicated that many rural cultures are and have been just as "secular" as the modern city? Secularity is not a phenomenon peculiar to the post-Reformation epoch, as Weber proposes, or even the post-Victorian period.

Given all these qualifications, we are still left with the reality of disenchantment as a receding of conventional faith and its commitments from the center of human life. Or better yet, what is ordinarily classified as a sacred category or sphere is transformed into a secular one and the secular is imbued with a sacred quality. The transcendent dimension, the vertical look, is not lost. It is horizontalized. And the horizontal is made transcendent. "Invisible religions" are created out of family-centeredness, sexuality, and class struggles. Modern forms of idolatry are created out of ancestors in Taiwan and Korea, kinship patterns in Africa, the "good life" in the United States.

B. Is there a point or points in this secularizing process where people can be said to be less "closed" to the good news that God reigns in Christ? Harvey Cox and the theologians of secularization, for example, make a great deal of the Bible's "desacralization" of nature as a divine entity. The biblical view of creation, to give one sample, is said to desacralize animism and its view of nature as a divine entity, the created order as filled with spirits and gods. Through this sort of biblical desacralization, the Creator and the creature are no longer defined by their interrelationship to nature; nature is disenchanted. The creation loses its divine character. What is the relation between this desacralization and the growth of the church? In urban settings still deeply entrenched in animism, in a religious world where humanity, nature, and God are strongly identified, can the gospel be the agent that opens the door not to secularism but to faith?

It is certainly true that animism in the industrial cities tends to lose its grips on its adherents. Respondents in two Xhosa-speaking communities in South Africa, one relatively rural and the other urban, were asked whether they had ever suffered a misfortune and, if so, if it were caused mystically (by witchcraft, sorcery, or ancestors). Seventy-three percent of the rural population attributed misfortune to such sources, but only 45 percent of those from the city did so. "Rural residents were far more likely than their urban counterparts to mention mystical causes."[39]

Gideon Sjoberg endorses this judgment on a wider scale. Magic, the religious instrument of animism, he argues,

> is not confined to preindustrial cities. It is practiced in the industrial milieu—but to a much lesser extent. As the traditional religions lose their effectiveness, magic itself becomes less pervasive, for the two tend to buttress each other. And industrial man comes to use science, rather than magic, to achieve his ends.[40]

Singapore's recent history underlines this same pattern of the disintegration of animism in the city. The breakdown of traditional Chinese religion, basically animistic at its core, is wide-spread, with people becoming either Christians or secularists.[41] And among those who are so-called secularists, there remains a very positive attitude to religion. In a study of secularist opinion in 1970, reports Keith Hinton, it was found that

> 83 percent were still interested in religion though not affiliated with any, 45 percent claimed they had had experiences of the presence of some deity in their lives, and 67 percent said they still sought help from some deity when they had a problem. Evidently the problem is not that of pure secularism, but rather of a people who have lost faith in the particular form of religion in which they were reared. They are not negatively disposed towards religion as such and are mostly open to a new, more credible expression of it. . . . Such an understanding of secularism in Singapore certainly throws a more rosy light on the evangelistic opportunity of the church. Most secularists, it would appear, have only become unaffiliated with religion because Christianity has failed to reach them with the truth.[42]

Hinton's conclusion is a bit more optimistic than I think we can be now about the secularization process. No definition of what he calls "pure secularism" is provided, no process of secularization is sketched. Instead of saying the secularists "are mostly open," is the situation not better evaluated by saying they are "less closed"? After all, judgments as to the winnableness of a people to the gospel are made not solely on the basis of how close they have come to Christ but also how far away they have moved. And secularization, in its basic thrust, is a movement away. A house swept clean of the demon of animism, unless filled with Christ, may find itself filled with three or five or seven demons of secularization.

Ultimately this question about where the gospel can best penetrate the secularization process cannot be answered until a prior question is studied. What is the process by which secularization takes place? Can we categorize the steps in such a process, creating something like a sliding scale? Will the scale be affected by an urban location? How? Is the scale to be a continuum moving from partial to unconscious to conscious secularism? How will we relate this question to suggested definitions of secularization, to the ideas of disengagement, disenchantment, and transposition? Are these related steps in the process, or complementary descriptions of the end-result? Evangelical scholarship has as yet done very little to examine this set of questions.[43] Until it's done, guesswork may lead to more mythmaking and urban fears.

3. Search for the felt needs behind secularization. What draws people to secularism as a way of life? What frustrates them about secularism as an answer to their questions? Are there social classes that seem more open to its influence? Answers to these queries can start us on the way to creative Christian responses and evangelistic strategies.

Keith Hinton's study of secularism in Singapore, for example, suggests more than just a negative attitude toward all religions generally. The vast number of secularists in that society are merely disenchanted with their old traditional religion. These people are not necessarily closed to the gospel nor even resistant to it.

Where can these people be found in the city? Look in the high schools and beyond, Hinton suggests.

> Chinese Religion shows a marked collapse as adherents obtain higher levels of education. The more superstitious Taoist form is the most vulnerable. Those who drop out of Chinese Religion either become Christians or claim "No Religion." . . . Protestants tend to gain most from the more highly educated and those with a slightly more philosophical Buddhist-type background.[44]

As you look at education, aim at science students. Hinton's research in Singapore indicates that this group converts

> to Christianity more readily than do arts students. One probable reason for this is that scientific studies are more powerful in undermining the presuppositions of the old world cosmologies. Another is that students of the humanities, exposed to the rationalistic philosophies and humanism of the West, find it more difficult to come to faith in Christ.[45]

113

All these instances point to what has been called a "positive" advantage of secularization: an erosion of traditional faiths and a search for new perspectives. Even the Muslim community, one of the most secure religions, can show this same erosion. We noted earlier the general stability of that faith, even after migration to the United States. However, even this now needs qualifications. New arrivals in Dearborn maintain their old Muslim values. But among those with a longer history in the United States there is "a very weak sense of religiosity." In this group very few conduct daily prayers and participate in the annual fast during the season called Ramadan. None conduct the pilgrimage ritual to Mecca, although some of them are wealthy. The rigid, traditional religion no longer seems fully appropriate for the new social environment. Religion for these generations fulfills the need for nationalist sentiments. From this group an "increasing number of persons . . . convert to Christianity. Although their number is very small, it is increasing from time to time."[46] Though the exact number is unknown, it does not seem to exceed 2 percent of the community.

Tim Matheny has discovered similar circumstances among Arab Muslims of the Middle East. There, in a category of people he designates "transitional" Arabs, one finds a people neither traditional nor modern. They are people in motion, people between. A majority of them were born in the villages and have since moved to the urban centers. In fact, it is the cities that have the highest concentration of Transitionals. Willing to reexamine their faith, open to innovation, they are less bound by a weakening Islamic stronghold. From them comes the largest number of converts to Christianity in the Middle East. In Lebanon 85 percent of the Muslims who have become Christians have been drawn from this group; in Jordan they comprise 74 percent, and in Egypt 68 percent.[47] Parallel to the secularists of Singapore, these transitional Arabs represent the vast majority of the high school and college students.

Is secularization more prominent in one social class than another? Do some of these classes tend to cluster around the place on a sliding scale of secularization that may leave them less "closed" to the gospel than other classes? This is another set of study questions for church-growth thinkers to analyze. In any case, wherever they are, it is not simply secularization alone that must be studied, but also the felt needs answered at that point by the secularizing process.

Among the working-class people, for example, according to a Lausanne Committee statement,

> there are many secularists whose felt needs refer more specifically to their experience of powerlessness, unemployment, environmental alienation, conflict between class solidarity and the expectations and pressures from the society as a whole. This is especially true in the context of the Third World. Christians should be engaged in solving these problems in their society. At the same time, these secularists need to sense and appropriate the power of the Holy Spirit through the salvation and Lordship of Jesus Christ in the midst of social insecurity and economic powerlessness.[48]

Again, many secularists are poor; secularization is not identifiable merely with the privileged. These poorer classes see Christianity either as a threat to their desire to become wealthy or as a means to keep them forever poor. The Christianity that will best touch them will require, in the Lausanne Committee's words,

> costly involvement from Christians who exemplify in their own lives the words they speak concerning Jesus and wealth. It is, sadly, often the actions of affluent Christian churches and leaders which reinforce the secularist poor in his position.[49]

And how large in our urban societies is that class of secularists now disillusioned with secularism itself? Disenchanted by the very process of disenchantment they have initiated, they find the promises of science and materialism empty and unfulfilled. They turn to the cults in the United States and to the occult in the Caribbean. The revival of animism in the city may point to this kind of frustration. Driven to the point of despair, the disenchanted secularists may be missed in our diagnosis of symptoms rather than the disease.

4. Develop a holistic ministry for the city. "The great problem stemming from increased urbanization," comments Howard Moody, a New York pastor, "is not that we do not have churches where the people are at or where the great masses are; rather, it is that the very folkways, activities and organizations of the church are irrelevant, sometimes actually anti-urban. . . . Our whole way of being the church in the 20th century is shown to be inadequate."[50]

Secularization as a process leaves no part of urban life untouched; politics, economics, education, and communication feel its impact. By contrast, in places like Latin America, "evangelicals have failed to teach and apply a New Testament social ethic, leaving no viable alternative other than Marxist revolution."[51] Church growth, separated from these areas without intention by a strategic concern for numerical and organic growth, can become ecclesiastical obesity. New life in Christ is commonly interpreted negatively—no smoking, no drinking, no parties, no fornicating—and a sharp line of demarcation is drawn between the church (everything good) and the urban society (everything bad). Secularization concerns itself with all of urban humanity; the church reduces itself to a private club for its members. Secularization moves through the totality and interrelatedness of human life; the church reduces the totalistic dimensions of the gospel to a narrowed focus on "saving souls." As a result, the church cannot respond to secularization; it has already capitulated to secularism in the form of a disengagement of the gospel from society.

A biblical call to repentance and saving faith in Christ does not call us away from the city; it calls us to live under the lordship of Jesus Christ in all areas of the city. Personal commitment to Jesus Christ is foundational. But on that foundation we erect a model house, demonstrating the full implications of the gospel for urban Christians where they live, work, and spend their time.

"Occupying until He comes" does not mean we board up our house in the city and stock it with enough spiritual food to last till the heavenly Landlord comes to break the siege. Between the coming of Christ and His coming again, the heirs of the earth and its cities are pilgrims and strangers. As pilgrims we share Christ's reproach as strangers in our own inheritance. But as heirs (Matt. 5:5) we exercise dominion over created things.

Our stewardship over creation, given in the garden (Gen. 1:28) and misshapen by sin (Gen. 3:17–19), is not reduced by the saving work of Christ to keeping the church lawn cut and mimeographing the Sunday bulletin. Creation and our stewardship of it are restored in Christ. The tyrant of the creation city was deposed at Calvary, and the cities of the earth have been given back to the rightful Sovereign and His people. Our calling now is to affirm His stamp of ownership on every building, street, and institution in the city. We are the city's voluntary tutorial staff, instructing the urban population to observe all that Jesus commanded (Matt. 28:19).

Edmund P. Clowney writes,

> The root evil of secularism as autonomy, independence from God, is emphasized in the Old Testament. It is worthy of note that the earliest evil after the fall, as presented in the book of Genesis, is not idolatry but primeval secularism. The civilization of the line of Cain is described as one of technical progress but one which is away from the face of the Lord and knows not the fear of the Lord. Lamech's song of the sword is a secular hymn that our century too has learned to sing. The tower of Babel is the great Old Testament symbol of the secular spirit as manifested in urban life. Only a divine interposition which broke the monolithic secular civilization of that period could preserve humanity from another divine judgment more complete than the flood.[52]

Even in Genesis, however, a response to secularism is suggested. It appears in terms of the "name" of humanity as over against the Name of God. Cain builds the first great city and gives it the name of his son Enoch (Gen. 4:17). This city of man's name appears again in the plain of Shinar: "Come, let us build us a city and a tower whose top may reach unto heaven, and let us make us a name" (Gen. 11:4). In contrast is the line of Seth, where people "call on the name of the LORD" (Gen. 4:26). And there is Abraham, the pilgrim of faith to whom God promises, "I will make thy name great" (Gen. 12:2). Abraham does not build his own city to establish his own name; he looks for "the city which hath foundations, whose builder and maker is God" (Heb. 11:10).

God's urban policy is more fully elaborated in the New Testament in Jesus' theme of the kingdom of God. Here we learn that "the name of the Lord" we are to spray-paint in graffiti on the walls of the world's cities is Jesus. The name of the Lord has become the name of Jesus, "the name which is above every name" (Phil. 2:9). To speak of Jesus is to speak of the kingdom. To believe in Jesus is to enter the kingdom (John 3:3, 5). To see Jesus casting out demons is to see that the kingdom has come (Matt. 12:28). The preaching of Jesus is the seed of the kingdom (Mark 4:3–14). His miracles are signs of the power of the kingdom unleashed (Luke 10:9). The kingdom, in short, is the rule of King Jesus.

As His kingdom disciples, we wait for His final coming and the consummation of that kingdom. And we wait by seeking first His kingdom and His righteousness (Matt. 6:33). What is the object of our quest? The church? Heaven? No, we are to seek God's righteousness—His sway, His rule, His reign in our lives and in our cities. In anticipation of His coming we pray, "Thy kingdom come" (Matt. 6:10). George Ladd writes,

> Are we praying for heaven to come to earth? In a sense . . . but heaven is an object of desire only because the reign of God is to be more perfectly realized than it is now. . . . Therefore, what we pray for is, "Thy kingdom come; *thy will be done* on earth as it is in heaven." . . . In my church, as it is in heaven . . . in my life, as it is in heaven. . . . The confidence that this prayer is to be answered when God brings human history to the divinely ordained consummation enables the Christian to retain his balance and sanity of mind in this mad world in which we live.[53]

Secularization is to be assaulted day by day by the piercing light of the kingdom.

This is not "unrealistic optimism" unless our theological perspective has no place for the reality of the kingdom now.[54] We achieve balance by remembering that we are "people between the times," racked by the tension that still exists between the kingdom of God and the last-ditch efforts of the kingdom of darkness in its death throes. In fact, the tension is stronger as we remember that everything now belongs to Him and nothing can exist outside of Him.

Our kingdom task in the city is not easy. Jesus came to redeem the whole cosmos, to "buy back" all things. But until He returns, our interim world is shared with non-Christians. We are called on to recognize their right to share with us in the development of the city. This right, however, is "founded, not in their fallacious assumption of human autonomy, but in the long-suffering goodness of God, who has not withdrawn from the sinner the world his wickedness has forfeited, but has given him its fruit in toil and suffering."[55] Sharing this right will make our struggle against secularization all the more difficult. But knowing that God has given the right (Matt. 5:45) and that one day it will be taken away must always make our struggle hopeful.

How is all this to be implemented in the life of the people of God?

— Crisis counseling centers in the cities of Australia with the victims of secularized society
— Christian labor unions in Indonesia to promote biblical teaching in regard to work and labor relations
— Professional theater groups in New York to reach the secularized culture shapers of the dramatic world
— Job banks established by networking city Christians to reach out to the marginalized and underemployed
— Revitalization of the office of deacon in the church from gatherer of church collections to distributor of Christian mercy and justice

    — Christian advocacy groups to speak for Jesus and the poor in government and human society[56]

Some have called this kind of program "pre-evangelism," doubtlessly out of an effort to see these actions as ground-breaking, preparatory service that can open doors for calling the non-Christian to Christ. But if these activities are accompanied by a clear-cut call to come to Jesus as Savior and Lord, as they should be, how can we call them *pre*-evangelism? If we continue to divide our Christian life into pre-evangelism and evangelism, how do we escape secularism-as-disengagement before we have even begun? The very process of secularization requires that we minimize this kind of distinction by maximizing the name of Jesus.

How would we describe the ministry of the Madison Avenue Christian Reformed Church in Paterson, New Jersey? Made up largely of generations of Dutch immigrants to the United States, the church in the 1950s began to face a changing city. Would they stay and minister to their growing black community, or would they leave for the suburbs? They decided to stay and be a community church.

Through the sixties, the church developed an intentional neighborhood and community ministry, described in these terms:

> In addition to the traditional congregational functions of worship and teaching, church members became involved in neighborhood nursery schools, youth groups, after-school centers and other programs; unlike the denominational exclusiveness of the past, these new ministries were directed to people outside the congregation in the predominantly black neighborhood.[57]

By the later sixties, black adults began to join the church. Within fifteen years this "bastion of white Dutch ethnicity" was transformed into a diverse, integrated, and multi-ethnic body of believers. Pre-evangelism had become evangelism.

Many of the congregation's outreach programs begun in the sixties still function. Church members are involved as a Bread for the World "covenant church" and help run a food pantry. Some members also work in a prison ministry and a local shelter for the homeless. More recently, members have joined the recently formed Paterson chapter of Habitat for Humanity, which plans to construct twenty homes over the next five years—a much-needed ministry in a city with severe housing problems.

The co-pastors—one black, one white—explain their philosophy of ministry in terms of the Calvinistic theology of their denomination. It is a faith that promotes holistic ministry. "An understanding of the Word and the deed go together," says one of the two. "We're trying to claim the lordship of Christ in all segments of life."

Whether this is pre-evangelism or evangelism may be, in the end, left to debate. That it speaks to the secularizing city can hardly be questioned.

NOTES

[1] Harvey Cox, *The Secular City* (London: SCM Press, 1965), p. 1.

[2] Ibid., p. 3.

[3] Timothy Monsma, *An Urban Strategy for Africa* (Pasadena: William Carey Library, 1979), p. 74.

[4] F. V. Tate, "Patterns of Church Growth in Nairobi" (Unpublished M.A. thesis, School of World Mission, Fuller Theological Seminary, 1970), p. 84.

[5] Benjamin Tonna, *A Gospel for the Cities* (Maryknoll, N.Y.: Orbis, 1982), p. 91.

[6] Paul Boyer, *Urban Masses and Moral Order in America, 1820–1920* (Cambridge: Harvard University Press, 1978), pp. 143–61.

[7] Reproduced in Robert D. Cross, ed., *The Church and the City, 1865–1910* (Indianapolis: Bobbs-Merrill, 1967), pp. 11, 15.

[8] Ibid., p. 28.

[9] William G. McLaughlin, *Modern Revivalism: Charles Grandison Finney to Billy Graham* (New York: Ronald Press, 1955), p. 119.

[10] Truman B. Douglass, "The Job Protestants Shirk," in *Cities and Churches: Readings on the Urban Church*, ed. Robert Lee (Philadelphia: Westminster, 1962), p. 90.

A CLARIFIED VISION FOR URBAN MISSION

[11] Francis DuBose, *How Churches Grow in an Urban World* (Nashville: Broadman, 1978), pp. 111, 117–19.

[12] Harvey Cox, *Religion in the Secular City* (New York: Simon and Schuster, 1984).

[13] Harvey Cox, "Religion in the Secular City: A Symposium," *Christianity and Crisis* 44, no. 2 (20 February 1984): 35.

[14] Cox, *Religion in the Secular City*, p. 268.

[15] Tonna, *Gospel for the Cities*, p. 93.

[16] Josef Gugler and William G. Flanagan, *Urbanization and Social Change in West Africa* (London: Cambridge University Press, 1978), p. 78.

[17] Atif Amin Wasfi, "Dearborn Arab-Moslem Community: A Study of Acculturation" (Unpublished Ph.D. dissertation, Michigan State University, 1964), pp. 128–41.

[18] Ira M. Lapidus, ed., *Middle Eastern Cities* (Berkeley: University of California Press, 1969), p. 47.

[19] Ibid., p. 140.

[20] Randall M. Miller and Thomas D. Marzik, eds., *Immigrants and Religion in Urban America* (Philadelphia: Temple University Press, 1977), p. xv.

[21] Russell Hale, *The Unchurched: Who They Are and Why They Stay Away* (San Francisco: Harper and Row, 1980), p. 173. Compare Earl Parvin, *Missions U.S.A.* (Chicago: Moody, 1985), p. 249.

[22] Charles L. Chaney, *Church Planting at the End of the Twentieth Century* (Wheaton: Tyndale House, 1982), p. 115.

[23] Ibid., pp. 102–5.

[24] William M. Newman, "Religion in Suburban America," in *The Changing Face of the Suburbs*, ed. Barry Schwartz (Chicago: University of Chicago Press, 1976), p. 267.

[25] Peter Glasner, *The Sociology of Secularization* (London: Routledge and Kegan Paul, 1977), pp. 1–2.

[26] Ibid., p. 7.

[27] Paul G. Schrotenboer, *The Meaning of Religion* (Toronto: Association for the Advancement of Christian Scholarship, n.d.), pp. 4–6.

[28] This is the point I have made earlier in "The Kingdom of God and the City of Man: A History of the City/Church Dialogue," in *Discipling the City*, ed. Roger S. Greenway (Grand Rapids: Baker, 1979), pp. 17–53.

[29] Edward C. Stewart, *American Cultural Patterns: A Cross-Cultural Perspective* (Washington: Society for Intercultural Education, Training, and Research, 1972), pp. 61–65.

[30] Peter Falk, *The Growth of the Church in Africa* (Grand Rapids: Zondervan, 1979), p. 426.

31 Waldron Scott, *Bring Forth Justice* (Grand Rapids: Wm. B. Eerdmans, 1980), p. 19.

32 Michael Toogood, "Stepping Back into the City," *Urban Mission* 2, no. 3 (January 1985): 9.

33 Chaney, *Church Planting*, p. 150.

34 Larry Shiner, "The Concept of Secularization in Empirical Research," *Journal for the Scientific Study of Religion* 6 (1967): 207–220.

35 C. W. Gates, *Industrialization: Brazil's Catalyst for Church Growth* (South Pasadena: William Carey Library, 1972), pp. 15, 24–26.

36 David Lyon, "Secularization: The Fate of Faith in Modern Society," *Themelios* 10, no. 1 (September 1984): 15.

37 Bryan Wilson, *Religion in Sociological Perspective* (New York: Oxford University Press, 1982), p. 42, quoted in Lyon, "Secularization: The Fate of Faith in Modern Society," p. 17.

38 Mary Douglas, "The Effects of Modernization on Religious Change," *Daedalus* 11, no. 1 (1982): 1–19.

39 William J. Hanna and Judith L. Hanna, *Urban Dynamics in Black Africa* (New York: Aldine, 1981), p. 60.

40 Gideon Sjoberg, *The Preindustrial City* (New York: Free Press/Macmillan, 1960), p. 281.

41 Keith Hinton, *Growing Churches Singapore Style: Ministry in an Urban Context* (Singapore: OMF Books, 1985), p. 85.

42 Ibid., p. 86.

43 *Christian Witness to Secularized People,* Lausanne Occasional Papers, no. 8 (Wheaton, Ill.: Lausanne Committee for World Evangelization, 1980), pp. 4–8.

44 Hinton, *Growing Churches Singapore Style,* p. 87.

45 Ibid., p. 88.

46 Wasfi, "Dearborn Arab-Moslem Community," p. 146.

47 Tim Matheny, *Reaching the Arabs: A Felt Need Approach* (Pasadena: William Carey Library, 1981), pp. 5–6.

48 *Christian Witness to Secularized People,* p. 18.

49 Ibid., pp. 14–15.

50 Quoted in Richard J. Tlapa, *The New Apostles: The Mission to the Inner City* (Chicago: Franciscan Herald Press, 1977), p. 73.

51 Roger S. Greenway, *An Urban Strategy for Latin America* (Grand Rapids: Baker, 1973), p. 117.

52 Edmund P. Clowney, "Secularism and the Christian Mission," *Westminster Theological Journal* 21, no. 1 (November 1958): 46.

53 George E. Ladd, *The Gospel of the Kingdom* (Grand Rapids: Wm. B. Eerdmans, 1954), pp. 21–23.

[54] An example of this very misunderstanding of the obligations of a present-future kingdom is evident in Arthur Johnston, "Essentials for Urban Ministry," *Alliance Witness* 120, no. 5 (27 February 1985): 9–10.

[55] Clowney, "Secularism and the Christian Mission," p. 51.

[56] For a book filled with such suggestions, consult Miriam Adeney, *God's Foreign Policy* (Grand Rapids: Wm. B. Eerdmans, 1984).

[57] "Serving Christ in the City," *Other Side* 21, no. 5 (July 1985): 8.

The Privatization Generalization: "It's Bigger Than Any of Us"

Chapter Five

The Privatization Generalization: "It's Bigger Than Any of Us"

American blacks call it "the System." It is more than burning crosses on the front lawn of the first black family in a white neighborhood. It is more than epithets of "nigger" hurled at a seven-year-old in a school playground. It is more than third-person-plural slurs about "them" and why welfare destroys "their" work initiative.

It is a "system," a social structure of urban society. It is a power arrangement based on wealth and whiteness that prevents the gap between the "haves" and the "have-nots" from shrinking. It is power disproportionately distributed and ethnocentric standards that define superiority.

Through the enculturation processes of white society, definitions of beauty are embedded into the black heart: "If you're white, you're all right; if you're brown, stick around; but if you're black, get back."[1] A white kindergarten child recites to his black playmate:

God made the nigger;
He made him in the night,
He made him in a hurry
He forgot to paint him white.

How do you change a "system"? Is it really enough simply to sit down with a white kindergarten child and tell him we don't use that kind of language? "Don't you say that!" Will that do it?

In Medellín, Colombia, many see the driving force of the political process as what is called *egoismo*. It is the tendency to subordinate all social and economic ends to personal gain or convenience. Related to it is *politiquería*, political maneuvering that tends to subordinate all policy-making goals to the personal rewards of the politician and his clique. It is selfishness systematized into a political structure. "Most of those who are involved in politiquería are individuals who participate in politics for no other reason than for the materialistic rewards which flow from the position obtained."[2]

How do you change, not simply selfish people, but a systemic structure built around selfishness?

It is hard for evangelicals, used to thinking of sin only on a personal level, to deal with it in any other shape. We think ordinarily of racists who need to repent. Where does one begin to repent of racism as a system? Selfishness we associate with an individual. How does one speak of an urban political system as selfish?

When we cannot deal with elephants walking over people, we create mentalities to bypass the issue. And we create appropriate proverbs to go with the mentality. We count the multiplication of urban systemic problems and pontificate, with Pollyannish optimism, "Saved individuals can change anything. One plus God is a majority." White Christians take note of the urban decline they have accelerated by their flight to the suburbs and, in self-defense and safety, respond, in their neighborhood Bible studies by the pool, "God honors those who are faithful to Him." Without a theological sense of anything larger than sinful individuals or saintly people, all they can do is resort to accusatory copouts. "People who don't work are lazy." "All that people buy with food stamps are champagne, cookies, and frozen dinners."

THE PRIVATIZATION GENERALIZATION

Behind much of this proverbial response to the sins of the city lies the danger of privatization. The church has clung to a private, individualistic notion of sin. The biblical dimension of solidarity, of complicity in sin, is theoretically recognized in the concept of original sin. But our cultural heritage of individualism minimizes the element of rebellion and antagonism against God and relegates it to the private, not the corporate, to the personal, not the structural dimension of human life. The terrible consequences of sin are drawn in terms of "the isolation, the loneliness of the guilty conscience which cannot shift the blame; it beams a narrow, intense light on the disruptive power of the sinful act to destroy the coherence, the meaning of a person's life."[3]

But this attitude neglects the fragmentation of sin which destroyed social relationships between Adam and Eve (Gen. 3:15–16) and between Cain and Abel (Gen. 4:7–8), that built urban societies in a conscious act of rebellion against the diffusionist plans of God (Gen. 4:16–17; 11:4). Social structures, as instruments of human interaction, are seen as sinful only in terms of the individuals who constitute them. Their holistic character, long an object of study for sociology and cultural anthropology, loses integrity under the force of individualistic compartmentalization.

Thus racism, when it is regarded as sin at all, becomes a sin of the individual. Evangelicals have even greater difficulty speaking of racism as a "social system" that also demands repentance. "Institutional racism," exemplified in the hiring record of major businesses on the fringe of a minority neighborhood, and the discriminatory practices of labor unions are harder to admit. Evil associated with a social structure is always less visible. It can permeate a system "carried out by well-meaning, good citizens. In fact, often executors of institutional racism are wholly unaware of their deleterious actions."[4]

Where can we see the fruits of this privatization of sin? In the loss of Christian hope for the city. Our evangelical commitment to the sovereignty of God knows that our Jonahs can be changed; it is not nearly so confident about our Ninevehs. God's grace can be bargained down to saving ten righteous people; but our faith stops short of a whole Sodom. On one occasion I talked to a Christian woman with deep commitments to changing the shape of her city. That week we had been horrified by a fire in a Philadelphia neighborhood that had killed ten people, the largest domestic tragedy in the city's history. The house had had no heat or water. My friend's eyes brimmed with tears and anger. "I practically pray through the evening news," she said. "What can we Christians do?" Realism in the face of the city's problems becomes pessimism under the weight of the privatization myth: little individuals cannot defeat massive urban evils.

Where can we see the fruits of this myth? In our continued bifurcation of evangelism and social responsibility. Evangelism is taken to mean "personal evangelism." But how will we link the personal focus of evangelism with the impersonal structures of society? Where will we find a place for social action in our evangelical understanding of discipleship as long as discipleship is reduced again and again to the "one on one" dimension?

In 1982 a Lausanne Consultation on the Relationship of Evangelism and Social Responsibility took us further along the road by speaking of the relationship in terms of "consequences," "bridges," and "partners."[5] But the bridge is shaky as long as evangelism is focused primarily on the individual alone and social responsibility centers its attention on the structural. The partners are said to be equal, but we all too often assume that one is more equal than the other. The privatization myth makes the difference.

Where can we see the fruits of this myth? In our personalized church agendas. The vision of the church as the body of Christ has been reduced to the church as the individual members of Christ. "Redemption" as a biblical word draws its significance from the socio-theological political history of Israel's deliverance from Egypt. "The Exodus from Egypt *is* the Old Testament redemption. . . . [The] individualizing and internalizing of sin finds no support in this history," writes Geerhardus Vos.[6] Nor does it in the New Testament, where Paul speaks of "new creation in Christ" (2 Cor. 5:17). The promised day of salvation is "not meant in an individual sense ('a new creature'), but one is to think of the new world of the re-creation that God has made to dawn in Christ."[7] Salvation is a matter of two worlds, not simply two individuals.

But cultural individualism has chipped away at this eschatological picture of two worlds. Calvinism and Arminianism divide on the place of the *individual* decision with respect to election. Which comes first in the life of the *individual*—regeneration or faith? Evangelists reduce the historical in salvation to the need for *personal* decisions for Christ. We sing, "Jesus loves me, this I know," and underline the *me* and not *Jesus*. Our methods of Bible study reinforce the pattern. In an inductive Bible study group, we are taught to ask repeatedly, "What does the Bible say *for me?*"

Moreover, the church's ethical agenda remains heavily individualized. In the evangelicals' not too distant past, moral concern was focused on questions of smoking, social dancing, and consuming alcoholic beverages. Poverty and racism were seldom discussed. Now abortion and prayer in the public schools replace earlier issues. And I suspect this is so because these issues also are easily transformed into personalistic categories. Justice issues are admitted into the evangelical Star Trek transmitter room and emerge with a heavy individualistic flavor. Under the bombardment of this emphasis, social questions are redefined. "Urban renewal" becomes a white euphemism for relocating the poor. "Public service" is the term we use when white suburbanites are on the receiving end; "welfare" is the term for the same process when we speak of the urban poor. "Reinvestment" is the term used by large banks to describe their policies of minimizing investments in areas whose racial structure is changing; "redlining" is what it means to the blacks moving into those areas.

Our individualized vocabulary is not big enough to handle the structural character of these verbalizations. We no longer see the urban crisis as "God's provision to the church to test our integrity, to force us to be honest, and to keep us from congratulating ourselves for a ministry abroad that we are loathe to practice at home."[8]

HOW DID WE GET THIS WAY?

"The city," writes Dale Cross, "offers to Christians the opportunity of presenting the pure gospel as it radically confronts every world system with the announcement that Jesus Christ is Lord."[9] What has happened to produce our mass-market boxing up and shipping out of leaven and salt for safekeeping away from the cities?

1. Our cultural captivity to the individualism of "the American Dream." In its crasser forms, it is reflected in the words of TV's Archie Bunker: "There's three great things that happens to a man during his lifetime: buying a house, a car, and a new color TV. That's what America is all about."[10] Horatio Alger's chronicles of American progress from rags to riches are the direct pipeline from Thomas Jefferson and Benjamin Franklin to "The Price Is Right." And Jefferson's message is the individualistic "pursuit of happiness."

From the millennial language of the Puritan vision, Jefferson extracted God as a figurehead deity and replaced Him with free, autonomous humanity pursuing its own aims in a free society. Tom Sine writes,

> Believing the individual to be inherently good, Jefferson insisted that he or she should have the power to decide how he

wanted to be governed and to violently tear down any government not in his own best interest—to decide whether God existed and to be the sole arbiter of conscience. Essentially he saw the autonomous self as the final authority in politics and religion. And he insisted that the supreme power of the individual had to be maintained not only by keeping government at an absolute minimum, but also by keeping economic systems as small as possible. Jefferson genuinely believed that if each person in the new order was given total freedom to pursue his or her self-interest, the common good would be the result.[11]

The economic theory of Adam Smith became another component of the Dream. Smith contended that if everyone were given absolute freedom to pursue his own economic advantage, the entire society would automatically progress. The "blind hand" of the free market would bring us to a better future.

"Rugged" individualism in American culture fed the frontier drive westward. And when industrialization was spawned in the nineteenth century, individualism fed an entrepreneurial spirit embodied in the "robber barons" of industry like John D. Rockefeller. The "free market" mentality has created what Pope Pius XI called the "great scandal" of the nineteenth century.

Amid the growth of the industrial cities of America, the church failed. They were still married to a land-tenure system that clustered their political and economic interests around the rural parish. They were still allied by mentality and outlook with the individualistic, entrepreneurial spirit. The churches accommodated the emerging middle and upper classes of the city and found themselves alienated from the new working classes. They saw little connection between poverty, urban blight, and rampant individualism. Roger Greenway comments,

> Rural-trained clergymen and middle-class laymen were united in regarding poverty as simply the consequence of individual sloth, and the Christian response, equally individualistic, came in the form of charity. Protestants of mid-nineteenth-century America were not yet prepared to think of evil in terms of social forces which worked against the poor, enslaved

them, and stamped out of them all vestiges of decency, morality and religion. The demons in societal structures were comfortably disguised.[12]

The myth of privatization disguised them.

The effect of this individualism is to see humanity as less than *homo sociologicus,* humanity in interaction with our fellows. It reduces the apostle Paul's plea not to let the society squeeze us into its mold (Rom. 12:2) down to Cain's query, "Am I my brother's keeper?" God lumps together private (Isa. 5:22) and public sin (5:23), personal and institutionalized evil (Amos 2:7), and condemns both equally. Individualism reduces injustice to a lack of personal charity.

2. Our class captivity to the elite few of "the American Dream." In all ideologies, visions for society are always the private possession of certain sectors of the populace, the self-defined elite. The North American Indian communities were the first to feel the sting of this power monopoly. The first charter of Jamestown in 1607 speaks of spreading Christianity and bringing "the infidels and savages . . . to human Civility."[13]

The history of the black in North America repeats this tragic flaw. "Lynchings, Jim Crow [laws] and sharecropping undercut Booker Washington's insistence that the American step-ladder of success awaited the black man of drive and patience. American civilization, with promises of freedom and mobility, tantalized the black man at the same time that it rejected him."[14] The Dream was unmistakably white.

After 1880, the dream turned from national vision to its worldwide destiny. The rise of the modern missionary movement drew much of its strength from this sense of Manifest Destiny. In 1885 a Congregationalist minister named Josiah Strong produced a book, *Our Country: Its Possible Future and Its Present Crisis.* It sold a then–phenomenal 175,000 copies. America, cried Strong, had survived its most crucial test in the Civil War and it had subdued a continent. But this progress caused new problems, he continued. With the West filled up and the nation industrialized, there would be new need for expansion in order to avoid catastrophe. The development of a new Anglo-Saxon world empire was the answer. In this empire we would see at last the coming of Christ's kingdom. This empire would be distinctively American, and missions were the first step. By contrast, he said, our cities had become the source of the evils of "rum, Romanism, and rebellion."

Strong's book served several purposes. It sparked missions enthusiasm in many of the nation's colleges and seminaries. It was pessimistic over the future of American cities and the growing non-Protestant immigrant populations filling them. And once more it called on the white Protestant elite to follow their dream.

In the years that have passed since Strong proclaimed his vision, his challenges have been accepted. But their dark side has also been disclosed. A book published in 1907 vividly portrayed the retreat of Protestantism from lower Manhattan. Forty Protestant churches abandoned neighborhoods below 20th Street, where two hundred thousand immigrants had moved in. The author puts the blame on both the churches and business greed.

> The filthy slum, the dark tenement, the unsanitary factory, the long hours of toil, the lack of a living wage, the back-breaking labor, the inability to pay necessary doctors' bills in times of sickness, the poor and insufficient food, the lack of leisure, the swift approach of old age, the dismal future—these weigh down the hearts and lives of vast multitudes in our cities. No hell in the future can be worse to them than the hell in which they now are.[15]

The title of the book, like its contents, aptly describes a perpetual dilemma: *Christianity's Storm Center: A Study of the Modern City*.

The pattern of abandoning the American city has continued. J. John Palen writes,

To WASP (white Anglo-Saxon Protestant) writers around the turn of the century, the sins of the city were frequently translated into the sins of the new immigrant groups pouring into the ghettos of the central core. Slum housing, poor health conditions, and high crime rates were all blamed on the newcomers. Those on the city's periphery and in the emerging upper-class and upper-middle-class suburbs associated political corruption with the central city. Native-born Americans tended to view city problems as being the fault of the frequently Catholic, or even Jewish, immigrants who inhabited the central-city ghettos.[16]

With the significant migration of blacks out of the South beginning with World War I, the elite class found new scapegoats for the sins of the city.

Developing concurrently with these patterns was the American missionary movement. It fed personnel largely to Third World rural areas where politically that was possible. Through the nineteenth century and into the twentieth, it continued to promote the American concept of Manifest Destiny through the key words "evangelization" and "civilization." One writer says,

> It was believed that both were supplementary and complementary: acceptance of the gospel through "evangelization" brought the desire and incentive to non-Western peoples to attain "Christian," that is, Western "civilization," while if "civilization" were stressed in initial contacts with these people, it produced understanding and acceptance of the gospel.[17]

Eventually, influential mission leaders began to question these equations. Rufus Anderson and Henry Venn called for "indigenous church" principles of self-propagation, self-government, and self-support. But both found themselves constantly at odds with their own missionaries in minimizing the need for white, Western "civilization" as a goal in missions. Even black Americans going to Africa in increasing numbers were often motivated by the same dream.[18]

What effect has this concept of Manifest Destiny played on our ability to perceive structural evil? A Ghanaian evangelical writes,

Foreign missionaries can no longer continue to work in Africa and assume that they come to do spiritual work and not to meddle in politics, for their very presence poses a problem. In the Africa of today the white man is still a reminder of the agony and chain of the slave trade of the dark years of political domination and economic exploitation, and the vicious circle of colonialism perpetuated in neo-colonialism. Western missionaries need to be aware, more than they have been in the past, of the griefs and sorrows of Africans, the very poor people to whom they are seeking to administer the healing power of the Gospel.[19]

Not long ago, twenty-four evangelical mission executives working in Latin America were polled about the relationship between evangelism and social action. Only two expressed any positive opinion about participating in movements seeking the transformation of government, industry, or other aspects of society. The other twenty-two insisted that evangelical witness should be directed toward soul-saving efforts and "discipling." Samuel Escobar, a Latin evangelical, links this reluctance directly to the American dream of Manifest Destiny.

How many missionary policies (today) are nothing but the reflection of the commercial and imperial practices of the *Pax Americana?* . . . If the message of the missionary has elements that foster a passive acceptance of the existing order, or a total refusal to deal with it critically, his presence is interpreted as active cooperation with the perpetuation of the system. This is even more true, of course, if missionary activity lends itself obviously to the service of business interests or the national interests of the missionary's country.[20]

3. Our ideological captivity to a geographical, and not a functional, definition of the city. Ideologies are our (often unconscious) pictures of what society ought to be like. They weave together values and beliefs into blueprints for the future of societal structures.

In 1938, Louis Wirth provided us with an ideological definition of the city "which became a persuasive, almost mesmerizing document that would dominate the field for the next twenty years."[21] Wirth attempted to define the universal, social elements of the city in terms of its internal demographic characteristics. The city is (1) a large, (2) dense, permanent settlement with (3) socially and culturally heterogeneous people. Size, morphology, and social complexity became the standard forms which were said to create urban life. These he saw as marking the barrier between rural and urban life.

Wirth was not optimistic about this way of life he called "urbanism." He saw it as weakening bonds of kinship and destroying the social significance of the family. He predicted the disappearance of the neighborhood and the undermining of the traditional basis of social solidarity.

In recent years, both sociologists and anthropologists have joined in sharply criticizing Wirth's geographical frame of reference. In his ideological picture of the city as a disintegrator, Wirth overlooked the role of the city as a social integrator. He underestimated as well the strength of the traditional ways of life. His whole model was said to be built on the assumption of the universality of the industrial city. The preindustrial city did not display this same quality of disintegration. Nor, in fact, did the industrial city as it began to be studied. His search for a universal city had a strong tendency, as ideologies do, to see the urban as a closed system.[22] And, moreover, in his case to see all cities as strikingly like Chicago.

The church, long linked by its history to the parish system of administration spawned by the rural, remains dominated by the geographical form of the city as a place. Some evangelical urbanologists do this in conscious imitation of the earlier ideas of Wirth and Redfield (see chapter 1) with little or no modification.[23] Others do it with little awareness of earlier theory. With little sensitivity to the sociologizing process of evil, they see cities only as places where size and population density increase the numbers of individual sinners. They are content with population statistics underlining their formal definitions of urbanism. The churches they plant in the cities often show little clear differences from those they have planted in rural areas. Their demographic studies in preparation for urban church planting pay little attention to political, ethnic, vocational, or social networks. They do not see the city as a whole. Contextual analysis of urban need is limited to a narrowed "religious" band, isolated from economics and class structures and neighboring networks.

More recently, through the impact of the Church Growth school, there is renewed interest in the ethnic networks of the city. But this too, as Orlando Costas has noted, can become a new form of atomism. It is not enough to isolate ethnic groupings. One can fail to see the interrelationships between "people groups" as such. Costas writes,

> It is a fact, especially in urban areas, that women and men usually belong to various groups at the same time. In such cases a natural cross-fertilization between groups takes place. They can influence and resist each other. Without an awareness of group linkage, it is not possible to assess realistically evangelistic progress or stagnation. . . . There also has to be awareness of the interconnecting links with other groups, for, as women and men exist in relationship, so do groups.[24]

What effect does this emphasis on the city as a place and not also as a process have on our perception of what has been called "structural evil"? It can maximize the internal character of sin and minimize its character as a cosmic revolution. Sin, to borrow the language of John Murray, "is a movement in the realm of spirit. But it drastically affects the physical and non-spiritual. Its relationships are cosmic."[25] It extends to the urban networks we created, and its acid eats away at their interrelationships. To diminish the networking processes of the city is to diminish our all-inclusive obligations to God and to promote our all-inclusive efforts to renounce those obligations.

BIBLICAL BEGINNINGS
AT DEMYTHOLOGIZATION

The myth of privatization, when consistently applied, undermines the call of the gospel to seek justice and peace in the city. The Reformed Ecumenical Synod declared,

> By divine fiat people always stand in a living network of relationships to other people. No human being is an island. Humans are contextual beings, societal creatures. Our lives are therefore integrally woven into a societal environment taking shape in a societal order. Individualism underestimates this associational character of human life within the created order by atomizing people, disrupting true community, and fragmentizing society. It lacks societal substance. It belies our intuitive sense, affirmed in creation and reaffirmed by Scripture (Acts 17:22–31, Ephesians 5:21–6:9), that there is a fundamental unity to the human race—a unified web of partnership relations.[26]

Minimizing the networking functions of the city reinforces this failure.

1. Corporate responsibility and structural evil. How can we break this mythological hold on our urban perspective? Some are seeking to do it by speaking of "social sin." More frequently the term "structural sin" is used. Behind the language is a commendable effort to deny that sin is only personal and is never therefore reflected in societal relationships or structures. Social, political, economic, and legal structures—indeed, the whole of life—are permeated with sin. Economic exploitation of the poor and political oppression of human beings by their fellowmen are urban realities that cannot be denied.

One of the virtues of a biblically constructed urban sociology lies precisely here. It highlights the complexities and contradictions of "a world adrift, characterized by competing attempts to construct social reality in a cosmos which has lost its proper centre."[27] It has helped expose some of the complex social dimensions of alienation, which biblically is called sin or evil and which finds its historical origin in the Adamic fall.

Finding the most effective terminology to describe this phenomenon is not easy. David Lyon comments that

> because sin is an intentional category, to do with action, it is misleading to speak of impersonal structures as being "sinful." Acts which flout God's directives for fulfilled human life may enter the constitution of structures, but that does not render the structures guilty before God.[28]

Lyon may not be doing equal justice to the unintentional character of sin, the "secret sins" (Ps. 90:8) known not even to those who commit them. But his concern is to point out that structures themselves can neither act nor be in themselves either good or evil. They are simply tools or mediums of human action (families, class-divided societies, churches) capable of either distorting or augmenting the Creator's intentions, of either enabling or restraining the divine purpose for human society.

Perhaps a more helpful designation is "structural evil" or "institutionalized sin."[29] Or, as David Kingdon suggests, "structural injustice."[30] Behind all these suggestions is a deep awareness of corporate responsibility, those obligations we have to discharge toward those with whom we are interrelated. John Murray says in this regard, "There are corporate entities which, as such, have responsibilities distinguishable from the strictly individual and personal responsibilities which belong to the persons comprised in these corporate entities."[31]

At the same time, such a corporate entity does not exist apart from the people who constitute that entity. Corporate credit or guilt never exists in abstraction. It devolves upon the personal and therefore becomes, in one way or another, personal responsibility. A table of nations speaks of Babel (Gen. 10:10), Assyria (10:11), and "the great city" (10:12), yet most of the names appear to be those of individuals.

The bearing of the name of its founder by a city or people

implied more than the mere identity of appellation. "Corporate extension" slipped easily from structural entity to individual and from individual to structural entity in covenant identity and solidarity. The election of the nation of Israel to be the people of God was related to the original call of righteous Abraham (Gen. 12:2). Corporate guilt brought defeat for the Israelites as a nation at Ai (Josh. 7:4–5). But personal guilt fell upon Achan for his violation of the divine ban on Jericho (Josh. 7:10–11). All Israel felt the wrath of God when Satan moved King David to number Israel (1 Chron. 21:1–8). While Jerusalem was capitulating to the Babylonians, the Edomites acted as informants on the side of the invader, looting and cutting off escape routes (Obad. 10–14). God acted against Edom for taking advantage of Judah (Mal. 1:4). But He also identified this providential punishment of Edom with Edom's father, Esau, and the divine favor on Jacob (Mal. 1:3). Pharaoh hardened his heart against the Lord. And God judged both Pharaoh and Egypt with him.

There is, then, a distinction between personal responsibility and corporate responsibility. But it is not the kind of distinction that absolves a person from complicity in corporate responsibility or abstracts corporate responsibility from an individual.[32] Richard Mouw comments,

> The Bible pictures all injustice and oppression as stemming from a posture of personal rebellion against the Creator. Corporate injustice and the neurotic patterns that characterize collective interaction are results of the institutionalization of this personal rebellion.[33]

2. Evil, injustice, and oppression. These institutionalizations of personal sinful patterns can come to have a life of their own. Isaiah's call to "cease to do evil" (1:16) is translated as learning to do good, seeking justice, reproving the ruthless, defending the orphan, pleading for the widow (1:17). Evil doings and an evil way are but the concretization of evil dispositions (Prov. 6:14; 21:10; Matt. 15:19).

And linking them all are not simply those acts we have grown accustomed to regard as evil—idolatry and apostasy (1 Kings 11:4–6), unfaithfulness and immorality (Deut. 13:5), adultery (Deut. 22:22, 24), and harlotry (Deut. 22:21). There is also the "evil" of "riches being hoarded by their owner to his hurt" (Eccl. 5:13), of the unjust oppression of a Pharaoh who demands bricks without straw (Exod. 5:19), of the afflicted and needy robbed by the strong (Ps. 35:10–12). Job reminds us that "to depart from evil is understanding," or wisdom (Job 28:28); he elaborates that definition with an autobiography defined in terms of delivering the poor who cry for help, being eyes to the blind, feet to the lame, a father to the needy (Job 29:12–16).

In short, structural evil is that which is perpetrated against the oppressed poor, widows, orphans, and aliens. The human righteousness required by God and established in obedience (Amos 5:24) has necessarily the character of a vindication of right in favor of the threatened and sinned against. "For this reason," states Karl Barth,

> in the relations and events in the life of His people, God always takes His stand unconditionally and passionately on this side and on this side alone: against the lofty and on behalf of the lowly; against those who already enjoy right and privilege and on behalf of those who are denied and deprived of it.[34]

God's vision for the city is a vision of paradise *shalom*. When "justice shall make its home in the wilderness and righteousness dwell in the grassland," only then will it be true that "righteousness shall yield *shalom* and its fruit be quietness and confidence for ever" (Isa. 32:16–17).

This vision God designed for the corporate life of His people. The law under which they lived was to reflect His character of justice and righteousness. They were "not laws for maintaining the status quo but rather have an impetus toward justice-making— especially in delivering the helpless—and the restoration of the created order."[35] Justice is defined in terms of our calling to protect the helpless (Deut. 10:17–18; 15:7–11). Bribery is condemned not simply because it perverts justice, but because it perverts justice owed to the poor and defenseless (Exod. 23:6–8; Deut. 10:17–18; 27:25; Isa. 33:15). Interest per se is not condemned, but interest that works against those without power and resources (Exod. 22:25–27; Deut. 15:7–11).

Against this background, oppression comes to the surface increasingly as "a basic structural category of biblical theology."[36] Oppressive power structures mean injustice (Eccl. 4:1; Ps. 72:1–4, 12–14; Mic. 3:1–3). Oppression enslaves (Ezek. 22:29), presses or squeezes (Exod. 3:9), and crushes (Amos 4:1; 5:11). Under the tyranny of oppression, the poor are humiliated (Ps. 94:5–6), persecuted (Ps. 129:1–2), and impoverished (Ps. 106:42).

And yet there is hope for society. In wrath God rewards the evil of the oppressor with evil itself (Judg. 2:11–15; 1 Kings 2:44). "Shall evil befall a city and the LORD hath not done it?" (Amos 3:6). God reciprocates; He rewards evil with evil. As divine retribution, evil is justice.

Beyond justice, mercy waits. "For you who fear my name the sun of righteousness shall rise, with healing in its wings" (Mal. 4:2). Jehovah will come, not merely to take sides with the oppressed in life's battles, but to dwell permanently with them (Isa. 57:15). The Lord will be a refuge for the poor, a refuge to the needy in his oppression (Isa. 25:4). The yoke that burdens will be shattered, the bar across the shoulders will be lifted, the rod of the oppressing one broken (Isa. 9:4).

Who will bring this liberation? The oppressed servant of Isaiah 53—He who endures oppression on our behalf, "smitten by God and oppressed" (53:4). "He was crushingly oppressed for our iniquities" (53:5, 10). With righteousness the stem of Jesse will judge the poor and decide with fairness for the afflicted of the earth (Isa. 11:4). A son will be given, a child will be born, a kingdom initiated and upheld "with justice and with righteousness" (Isa. 9:6–7).

Bethlehem cries out, This day of justice has dawned.

Christmas for Mary heralds not simply a gospel of consolation but of the kingdom renewal of justice. "He has brought down rulers from their thrones but has lifted up the humble. He has filled the hungry with good things but has sent the rich away empty" (Luke 1:52–53).

Nazareth cries out, The day of jubilee, of restoration, is fulfilled (Luke 4:17–21). And Calvary and the redeeming death of the servant becomes the Day of Atonement that initiates the jubilee (Lev. 25:9). God's final answer to personal and structural sin and evil becomes a cross, "a cosmic lightning rod: on the cross God's son suffered hell and all other consequences of God's anger over human injustice."[37] The pervasiveness of sin in our world, the extent to which the whole structural orders of society are corrupted by injustice, the enormity of our private misdeeds and social violence against our neighbor, can be measured only by the depth of the vicarious penal restitution of the oppressed servant at Calvary.

3. A new society and a new creation. In the light of that cross and the vindication of the servant at the Resurrection, His children are called to resist evil (1 Thess. 5:22; 1 Peter 3:10–12). "Hate what is evil, hold fast to what is good" (Rom. 12:9).

The Cross becomes the boundary between the church and the world, addressing the world as a society under God's wrath and without the capacity for self-healing. At the same time, there are images of the church in the New Testament that indicate the Cross is "also a bridge for constant two-way traffic."[38]

Through metaphors like the church as "the new creation" (2 Cor. 5:17; James 1:18), we see the Christian society as a new beginning for cosmic society. The church as "the new humanity" (Eph. 4:24; Col. 3:10) furnishes us with a self-image in which the church is set in a cosmic, social context. The church as "new humanity" becomes "ideally an approximate picture of what the world ought to be; the world, on the other hand, is what the church would still be were it not for the reality of grace and of restoration to divine obedience."[39]

What do we see when we visualize the church as the firstfruits of God's creatures, the light of the world (Matt. 5:14; Phil. 2:15), the new humanity (Eph. 2:15)? As the firstfruits of the creation, the church is a paradigm of God's will for all of humanity and its societal structures, a promise of greater things to come. In the faces of the church we behold the pioneers of what human society collectively could have been and in Christ should be before the face of God. As the new humanity, the church is called to incarnate the renewed human society living in accord with God and with each other. The church is to be a societal model, God's demonstration community of institutionalized righteousness.[40] The church is "not the clerical vassal of the social order but the vanguard and vehicle of the coming kingdom."[41] She is the sign of the new order of the Spirit, the bearer of structural justice.

Given these images of the church, why does the body of Christ in the city look more like a spectator than a servant and dispenser of justice? Because our vision of "church" is dominated by what is and not by what should be. Before we say "church" we have been thinking of something specific, of a certain company of people on a certain street in a certain city, of others like ourselves within an organization that has very tangible denominational boundaries and a very concrete history. To this reality we attach the images of the new humanity and the new creation, prooftexting in a supportive way the patterns of ministry shaped by our society. The images become commendatory ways of recommending existing realities, not instruments for rebuilding new models. The church thus becomes a contemplative social structure, not a world-formative one.[42] Our picture has been shaped by a look backward and not an eschatological look forward.

The focus of the New Testament is quite the reverse. The shape of the church and its calling in the city as "firstfruits" is the shape of the present, proleptic beginning of the end. It is an institution that has identified by faith the coming of the kingdom of God in Christ. In His redeeming work, it has seen the "eruption of an overwhelming and just power" that will, with His return, reconstitute human societies as the single society of the divine warrior through the agency of His triumphant Son.[43] And the task of the church, until that glorious day, is to be co-workers with God in the formation of the new creation. This is why the church is not content merely to change individuals: God is not so content. One day soon He will create a wholly new environment in which the righteousness of His people will shine.

The church is to press toward this eschatological goal thrust on us by God's work and by His design and final execution. We labor in hope for a city of God in which justice and *shalom* are realized. We labor in the knowledge that God alone can build it. But, in Pannenberg's words, our "satisfaction is not in the perfection of that with which we begin but in the glory of that toward which we tend."[44]

What will be the criteria by which the church tests all political and social institutions and practices? What do they do to the poor? In 1891, Abraham Kuyper expressed it this way:

> When rich and poor stand opposed to each other, [Jesus] never takes His place with the wealthier, but always stands with the poorer. He is born in a stable, and while foxes have holes and birds have nests, the Son of Man has nowhere to lay His head. . . . Both the Christ, and also just as much His apostles after Him as the prophets before Him, invariably took sides *against* those who were powerful and living in luxury, and *for* the suffering and oppressed.[45]

What will be the instrument of the church in effecting this change? Not simply charity but also justice. Charity is episodic, justice is ongoing. One brings consolation, the other correction. One aims at symptoms, the other at causes. The one changes individuals, the other societies. One cries out in the name of Jesus, "I love you." The other adds, "Because I love you, I do for you what is right."

NOTES

[1] William H. Grier and Price M. Cobbs, *Black Rage* (New York: Bantam, 1969), p. 66.

[2] Wayne A. Cornelius and Robert V. Kemper, eds., *Metropolitan Latin America: The Challenge and the Response* (Beverly Hills, Calif.: Sage Publications, 1978), p. 138.

[3] Patrick Kerans, *Sinful Social Structures* (New York: Paulist, 1974), p. 61.

[4] David Claerbaut, *Urban Ministry* (Grand Rapids: Zondervan, 1983), p. 135.

[5] *Evangelism and Social Responsibility: An Evangelical Commitment,* Lausanne Occasional Papers, no. 21 (Wheaton, Ill.: Lausanne Committee for World Evangelization, 1982): 21–24.

[6] Geerhardus Vos, *Biblical Theology* (Grand Rapids: Wm. B. Eerdmans, 1948), p. 124.

[7] Herman Ridderbos, *Paul: An Outline of His Theology* (Grand Rapids: Wm. B. Eerdmans, 1975), p. 45.

[8] Craig Ellison, ed., *The Urban Mission* (Grand Rapids: Wm. B. Eerdmans, 1974), p. 1.

[9] Dale W. Cross, "Evangelizing America's Cities," in *The Urban Challenge,* ed. Larry L. Rose and C. Kirk Hadaway (Nashville: Broadman, 1982), p. 102.

[10] Spencer Marsh, *God, Man and Archie Bunker* (New York: Bantam, 1976), p. 73.

[11] Tom Sine, *The Mustard Seed Conspiracy* (Waco, Tex.: Word, 1981), p. 77.

[12] Roger S. Greenway, *Calling Our Cities to Christ* (Nutley, N.J.: Presbyterian and Reformed, 1973), pp. 23–24.

[13] Ronald D. Pasquariello, Donald W. Shriver, Jr., and Alan Geyer, *Redeeming the City: Theology, Politics, and Urban Policy* (New York: Pilgrim, 1982), p. 139.

[14] Donald F. Roth, "Grace Not Race: Southern Negro Church Leaders, Black Identity and Missions to West Africa, 1865–1910" (Unpublished Ph.D. diss., University of Texas at Austin, 1975), p. 3.

[15] Quoted in Pasquariello et al., *Redeeming the City,* pp. 142–43.

[16] J. John Palen, *The Urban World* (New York: McGraw-Hill, 1981), p. 71.

[17] Sylvia M. Jacobs, ed., *Black Americans and the Missionary Movement in Africa* (Westport, Conn.: Greenwood, 1982), p. 14.

[18] Walter L. Williams, *Black Americans and the Evangelization of Africa, 1877–1900* (Madison: University of Wisconsin Press, 1982), pp. 85–124.

[19] Quoted in Waldron Scott, *Bring Forth Justice* (Grand Rapids: Wm. B. Eerdmans, 1980), p. 156.

[20] Samuel Escobar and John Driver, *Christian Mission and Social Justice* (Scottdale, Pa.: Herald, 1978), pp. 76–77.

[21] James L. Spates and John J. Macionis, *The Sociology of Cities* (New York: St. Martin's, 1982), p. 47.

[22] For a lengthy criticism of Wirth's ideas, consult Ulf Hannerz, *Exploring the City* (New York: Columbia University Press, 1980), pp. 65–76.

[23] An example of this heavy indebtedness is found in the thinking of Francis DuBose. Compare his book *How Churches Grow in an Urban World* (Nashville: Broadman, 1978), pp. 32–35; and F. M. DuBose, "The Practice of Urban Ministry: Urban Evangelism," *Review and Expositor* 80, no. 4 (Fall 1983): 515.

[24] Orlando Costas, *Christ Outside the Gate* (Maryknoll, N.Y.: Orbis, 1982), p. 166.

[25] John Murray, *Selected Lectures in Systematic Theology*, vol. 2 in *Collected Writings* (Edinburgh: Banner of Truth Trust, 1977), p. 72.

[26] *RES Testimony on Human Rights* (Grand Rapids: Reformed Ecumenical Synod, 1983), p. 21.

[27] David Lyon, *Sociology and the Human Image* (Downers Grove, Ill.: InterVarsity, 1983), p. 49.

[28] Ibid., p. 135.

[29] Scott, *Bring Forth Justice,* p. 214; also, Ron Sider, *Rich Christians in an Age of Hunger* (Downers Grove, Ill.: InterVarsity, 1975), p. 133.

[30] David Kingdon, "Some Questions About Structural Sin," *Christian Graduate* 33, no. 2 (July 1980): 13.

[31] Murray, *The Claims of Truth*, vol. 1 in *Collected Writings* (Edinburgh: Banner of Truth Trust, 1976), p. 273.

[32] Ibid., p. 274.

[33] Richard J. Mouw, *Politics and the Biblical Drama* (Grand Rapids: Wm. B. Eerdmans, 1976), p. 49.

[34] Karl Barth, *Church Dogmatics,* vol. 2, pt. 1 (Edinburgh: T and T Clark, 1955), p. 386.

[35] William Dyrness, *Let the Earth Rejoice!* (Westchester, Ill.: Crossway, 1983), p. 64.

[36] Thomas D. Hanks, *God So Loved the Third World* (Maryknoll, N.Y.: Orbis, 1983), p. 4.

[37] Ibid., p. 117.

[38] Paul S. Minear, *Images of the Church in the New Testament* (Philadelphia: Westminster, 1960), p. 243.

[39] Carl F. H. Henry, *A Plea for Evangelical Demonstration* (Grand Rapids: Baker, 1971), p. 121.

[40] Robert Recker, "The Redemptive Focus of the Kingdom of God," *Calvin Theological Journal* 14, no. 2 (November 1979): 178–79.

[41] Jim Wallis, *Agenda for Biblical People* (New York: Harper and Row, 1976), p. 133.

[42] For an excellent analysis of this phenomenon, consult Nicholas Wolterstorff, *Until Justice and Peace Embrace* (Grand Rapids: Wm. B. Eerdmans, 1983).

[43] Dyrness, *Let the Earth Rejoice!* p. 189.

[44] Wolfhart Pannenberg, *Theology and the Kingdom of God* (Philadelphia: Westminster, 1969), pp. 80–81.

[45] Abraham Kuyper, *Christianity and the Class Struggle* (Grand Rapids: Piet Hein, 1950), pp. 27–28, 50.

The Power Misunderstanding: "You Can't Fight City Hall"

Chapter Six

The Power Misunderstanding: "You Can't Fight City Hall"

"Things don't work right in the city," says a black mother from North Carolina. She has spent seven hours waiting for help in a public health clinic in Philadelphia while cradling her two-year-old daughter with a temperature of 103. A policeman in Chicago stands over the body of a sixteen-year-old boy shot to death in a war of street gangs. "My boy is that age," he says quietly. "But what can you do? It's the city."

A seventeen-year-old prostitute, one year on the streets in Seoul, tells of her coming to the city and her failure to find a way. "I didn't know where to go and what to do. It was all so big, so overwhelming!" The city originally had been her hope for a good life. Now it had become her exploiter. The "last chance" had become "no chance."

Cities are centers of power in the world. But for many, power means manipulation and marginalization. The pattern is not a new one.

The founding of Ur of the Chaldees (Gen. 11:28; 15:7) is

dated from before 4000 B.C. A thriving city with dependent towns and villages, it offered protection and food to its satellite "daughters" in exchange for bureaucratic organization, military force, and political power. Towering above all other buildings, the dominant feature of the city was the *ziggurat,* a temple tower, the symbol of not only religion but religious power. At the summit of its three-tiered terraces was the shrine to the moon god, reminding the surrounding countryside that the priest-king rulers of this city derived their power from the gods; these priest-kings alone were able to perform rituals thought vital for the fertility of the land and its people. From the shadow of its exploitative religion, Abraham was called to look for another kind of city (Heb. 11:8–10).

Ur was typical of the cities of the Ancient Near East. Gideon Sjoberg explains,

> Each city was ruled by a king who was considered a representative of the city's tutelary deity and thus its chief priest. Inasmuch as the land that supported the city was considered to belong to the chief god, the farming populace was expected to return to him part of the "surplus" crop; this tribute was held by the city's main temple where it was stored in the granaries attached to it. In all probability it was the chief sustenance of the city's ruling group.[1]

The city had become what Lewis Mumford describes as "a new symbolic world, representing not only a people, but a whole cosmos and its gods."[2] The king became a mediator between heaven and earth, incarnating in his own person the fusion of divine right and power. Power—cosmic, divine, and human—merged into one and was the mainstay of the new city.

Nowhere is the evil side of that power syndrome in the city more apparent than in the biblical record and especially in the city that personifies the power of the Near Eastern cultures: Babylon. The roots of that city are traced to Nimrod, "the world's first great conqueror" (Gen. 10:8, TEV). The culmination of his tyranny and despotism is the city of Babel and its tower (Gen. 11:4). There on the plain south of the site of modern Baghdad, Nimrod called with power for a city whose tower would "reach into heaven." God promised Abraham that He would make his name great; Nimrod's city builders, by contrast, would make their own name great (Gen. 11:4).

The message of urban tower power is repeated throughout the Old Testament in the imagery of the Babel *ziggurat*. Israel prepared to cross the Jordan in order to dispossess "great cities fortified to heaven" (Deut. 9:1; cf. 1:28). Jeremiah reminded his audience that "though Babylon should mount up to heaven and though she should fortify her strong height, yet destroyers would come from me upon her, says the LORD" (Jer. 51:53).

As the city grew into an empire, the ruthlessness of her power was challenged by the prophets. "You showed them no mercy," the Lord warned them. "Even on the aged you laid a very heavy yoke" (Isa. 47:6). The city made strength her god (Hab. 1:11). She was scourge (Jer. 27:1–28:17), hammer (Jer. 50:23), the mistress of kingdoms (Isa. 47:5), the self-styled "eternal queen" (Isa. 47:7). In her arrogance "the oppressor" dispenses "pain and turmoil and harsh labor" (Isa. 14:3–4).

The imagery continues into the New Testament. In the Book of Revelation the eschatological battle of the centuries pits Babylon against the New Jerusalem. The harlot of power that intoxicates the nations like a golden cup (Isa. 51:7) will be brought to ruin (Rev. 17:16). God's divine measuring scale gives her as much torture and grief as the glory and luxury she gave herself (Rev. 18:7). The plagues of her power—death, mourning, and famine— turn upon their source. The systems of urban power become witnesses to the urban downfall.

> Business operates for the city, industry is developed in the city, ships ply the seas for the city, luxury and beauty blossom forth in the city, power rises and becomes great in the city. There everything is for sale, the bodies and souls of men.[3]

And in one hour it is gone, leaving kings and merchants and seamen terrified. "Woe! Woe, O great city, O Babylon, city of power!" (Rev. 18:9, 16, 19).

How will we read these symbols? Is Babylon another name for Rome? Perhaps so. But what was Rome to the early church? Coercive government, human wickedness, culture gone bad, human dominion under the power of Satan. Towers that reach up to heaven, defiant shouts of "Is this not mighty Babylon that I have built?" Wealth transformed by greed into luxury and sensuousness, power usurped and gone bad.

POWER, MANIPULATION, AND THE MODERN CITY

The leap in time from Babylon to Boston and Beirut leaves in its wake the systemic collusion of religion and power. The mayors of Chicago and Kinshasa do not exercise their power because of their religious credentials given them by the gods. But the connections of power and manipulation in the city seem strong to many.

To the urban poor of Latin America, the history of their cities is the history of landowner elitism and the marginalization of landless masses. In 1561, Lima had a population of 99,600 inhabitants. Of these, only 40 were landowners. It was this group "who monopolized means for acquisition of wealth, governmental positions, and prestige. . . . Elites of rapidly growing cities governed them largely in their own interests with a measure of respect for the interests of Crown and Church, but without much concern for those of the new urban masses."[4] Power monopolies established early in the colonization of Latin America transformed Spanish latecomers, mestizos, and native Indians into disenfranchised masses. They were permitted to fend for themselves in the city under the benign indifference of the authorities.

Marginalization has continued as the poor have flooded the contemporary city. By 1970, Guadalajara had a population of more than one million—36 percent of its state's total census. At least 60 percent of the city lived below the poverty line. Its housing "still reflects a condition of absolute deprivation among the poor."[5] Mexico City in the same year had 110,000 unemployed and 350,000 underemployed. Marginalization, Alan Gilbert explains, is created by

> a vicious circle of low capital, low training, shortage of remunerative work opportunities, and low incomes. Only a minority with considerable luck, talent or initiative can break out of this situation, and the strength of a minority is often conditional on the relative stagnation of a great majority.[6]

Surprisingly, the response of the poor to this process is said to be neither anger nor apathy. Latin American urban families in search of economic survival and a minimum of security see revolution and drastic replacement of old elites by new ones as farfetched and undesirable.[7] But the pain remains.

A shanty town woman in São Paulo writes in her diary of a daily battle with hunger.

> *May 15 [1955].* This is how I see São Paulo. The governor's palace is the living room. The mayor's office is the dining room. The city is the garden. The *favela* is the place where the rubbish is dumped.

> *Dec. 25, Christmas.* José [her son] came back with a stomachache. I know why: he ate a spoiled melon. Today they dumped stuff near the river. I don't know why those idiot merchants throw away the rotten food near the *favela;* the small children see it and eat it. I think the merchants are playing with the people, like Caesar when he tortured the Christians. But the Caesars of today are worse than the Caesar of the past. The Christians were being punished for their faith, but we for our hunger. At that time those who didn't want to die had to stop loving Christ, but we can't stop needing to eat.[8]

The pattern is repeated in Asia. The "have-nots" enter the growing cities from the villages and smaller urban communities, expecting to become the "haves." But the contrasts remain—slum and suburb, rich and poor, class and caste. Few political parties take sustained and systematic interest in the needs of the poor. In Seoul and Bangkok, as in Panama City, a few months before national elections, the candidates hold political rallies and take walking tours through low-income urban districts. Sometimes food and clothing are distributed. Party platforms often include proposals for low-cost housing and employment-generating public works. But too often the plans are merely unkept promises, and the attempts that are made are sporadic, half-hearted, and poorly executed. With some exceptions, even the Communist party shows little interest in the marginalized and the urban poor. "A good deal of communist support frequently comes from comparatively skilled and well-educated workers, including white-collar groups."[9]

Out of this experience, the urban poor learn one of two things about access to power: "You have to know the right patron or have the right amount of money"; or, on a more discouraging note, "You can't fight city hall."

The Africans' respect for power has never been limited to the city. Timothy Monsma writes,

> Whether that power be temporal power wielded by a chief or king, or whether it be spiritual power wielded by gods, ancestors, witches, or fetishes, powers are to be respected. The person who migrates to the cities carries this respect for power with him. The power of gods, ancestors, witches, and the fetishes may fade somewhat in the urban environment, but there are other powers to contend with—the power of the police and the army, of government officials and tribal organizations.[10]

In the rural area one gains access to power through religious ritual. In the city the channel becomes political and economic manipulation. Urban Africa becomes an opportunistic society. Chinua Achebe, the famous novelist, sums up the proverbial reality, "A common saying . . . after Independence was that it didn't matter *what* you knew but *who* you knew. And, believe me, it was no idle talk."[11]

Migrants to the United States in the nineteenth century quickly learned the lesson Achebe underlines for Africa. During the half-century after the Civil War, nearly twenty-five million came to the United States. By the end of the century, New York could boast that it had more Italians than any other city except Rome, more Greeks than any other city except Athens, more Jews than any other city in the world.

As the cities grew by leaps and bounds, the problems grew faster than those in urban government could solve. Guidance through the maze came from political bosses and the businessmen who used improvements as a means of lining their pockets.

> The most disheartening aspect of city life was the corruption in politics. The city was a shapeless conglomeration of clashing races, nationalities, religions, and classes, but most of its dwellers exercised the vote. As a politician, the aim of the political boss was to win votes, but aside from that he performed the function of bringing some order into urban confusion, both for the good of the citizens and to serve the bourgeoning industries. Order meant welding together the inchoate masses. This the political boss achieved by giving out five-dollar gold pieces for votes and organizing picnics and parades, but even more by furnishing the social services that public opinion did not yet permit states and cities to provide. He provided for the widow and orphan, aided the man out of work, helped the boy in trouble with the law, and looked after the newly landed immigrant.[12]

The money that provided these services came from percentages of the salaries of municipal employees and cuts from contracts awarded to city builders. The boss found ways to get around the law or to change it—for a price. Since you couldn't fight city hall, you hired it.

One group, however, found it difficult—then and now—to buy into the system. The American black felt the full weight of urban racism against "nonwhites." With a deep sense of powerlessness shaped by centuries of slavery, the black's self-image was shaped by insecurity as a way of urban life.

"Hold fast to dreams, for if dreams die, life is a broken-winged bird that cannot fly," wrote black poet Langston Hughes.

But the urban experts who surveyed New York's Harlem neighborhood in 1978 came to a sobering conclusion: "Harlem is now the broken-winged bird," one said. "Its dreams are dead; its people are despairing and worse off than they ever were. The high hopes of the 1960s are gone."[13]

Harlem is not alone. Washington, D.C., is described by one evangelical as "actually two cities inhabiting the same territory." There is official Washington, whose chief characteristic and commodity is power. "People are here because they have it, they want it, or just like to be close to it. Here are the powerful, the power hungry and the power groupies."[14]

The other Washington is mostly black and poor. Its leading characteristic is powerlessness. It is the Washington of unemployment, drugs, alcohol, crime, and despair. Four out of ten black students in schools like those in Washington will not get jobs. Police often simply contain or tolerate urban crime unless the victims are white.

Out of such cities comes black distrust in the power structure. Research published in 1982 reinforces this picture. Of those surveyed, more than nine out of every ten blacks showed some degree of concern over their capacity to alter the social structure in ways that would render it more compatible to black goals. More than one-fifth did not believe that things will get better in the future. In Boston, blacks saw the city as extremely racist and prejudiced. More than half of those surveyed (54.4 percent) indicated "high" distrust in the power structure.[15]

Black responses to powerlessness take various forms. All are lifestyle strategies oriented to coping as a survival attitude. David Claerbaut explains,

> The first is an expressive lifestyle. This is a flashy style, which externally denies poverty. It may include gaudy dress, a financed car, and other material props to support the joking, impulsivity, and spontaneity at the core of this mode. Often, this expressiveness gives rise to drunkenness, drug addiction, and sexual promiscuity in an effort to appear "cool" and stylish.[16]

The failure of this style can turn the black to a second strategy: violence. Out of rage with the hopelessness and degradation of poverty, a poor person turns to fear-producing activity in which others are forced to meet his or her needs. Murder (more often black against blacks), muggings, teacher and student assaults, and gang conflicts become barometers of marginalization.

On March 19, 1935, there was a riot in Harlem that marked the first time blacks in the United States had initiated violence on a large scale. It was a ghetto riot, not a race riot. Looters pillaged food and clothing stores owned by both races and fought the police, but they did not attack whites. By the end of the day, one hundred people were injured and property damage reached two million dollars. According to one observer, it was a frenzy of looting in which "crowds went crazy like the remnants of a defeated, abandoned, and hungry army."[17] The pattern had begun. The pain must be exorcised.

A third lifestyle is the depressive strategy. In it there is a scaling down of one's goals to the levels of necessity. A defeatist strategy, its proverbs are "Live and let live" and "Don't bother me and I won't bother you." The colonialist message to the colonized, "You are inferior," is finally interiorized. The black comes to believe he or she is inferior, as a shield against further disappointment and heartache.

Verley Sangster, national director of Young Life Urban Ministries, epitomizes it in his description of Natalie, a beautiful sixteen-year-old. She could be a successful model, but "she's always so down on herself. She has no hopes beyond surviving today . . . no dreams, no goals, no future."[18] The two stand on a street corner one quiet summer evening talking.

"Natalie, what do you want to do with your life?"

With a sigh of resignation she looks up at the street sign. "I feel like there's a gate across Washington Street and I can't go any place beyond here . . . and what's here but a lot of drugs and stuff."

POWER, MARGINALIZATION, AND THE CHURCH

In this struggle between power and powerlessness, how is the church perceived by the marginalized? How does the church view the marginalized? Are they an "unreached people" on our evangelistic agenda?

In general, the picture is discouraging. As one samples opinions among the blue-collar, industrial workers and unskilled laborers, the gap between their lives and the church is perceived as growing wider and wider. Around the world, few find their way into the church. Kuo-shan Tsai, general secretary of the Taiwan Industrial Evangelical Fellowship from 1979 to 1983, comments on six years of ministry among the three million industrial workers of Taiwan's island community:

> I discover that over 95% of them are aware of Christianity. Generally speaking, they tend to be comparatively open-minded toward Christianity due to the rapid change of their life style. They have a positive attitude toward the Gospel when it is presented to them. Nevertheless, this does not mean that they are friendly toward Christians or wish to join local churches. On the contrary, they complain that many Christians are self-centered, materialistic and proud. They also feel that the message of local churches is irrelevant to their daily life, and most programs are geared towards the needs of the intellectuals or the middle class.[19]

In Singapore, the gap looks as wide. There is a clustering of Christians in the upper levels of the community. In 1980, 10.3 percent of the total population were Christians. But taking a census of job descriptions reveals more startling information. Among those working as professional and technical persons, the Christian percentage reaches 28 percent. Of those in managerial and administrative positions, 24 percent are Christians. A significant 17.4 percent of those in clerical work are also Christians. All these figures are much higher than the national average. Consider the blue-collar, production industries. Here 40.2 percent of Singapore's workforce is found—yet only 4 percent are Christians.[20]

The picture in the Philippines seems better. The largest of the four groups in Filipino society, larger than the three others combined, is the *tao,* or common person. In this category we find the day laborer, carpenter, market vendor, household servant, tenant farmer, and fisherman. Most Filipino Protestants come from this group.

At the bottom of the society's economic scale are the very poor, the squatters and slum dwellers of Manila. Here is the largest block of unreached peoples. Here in poverty-ridden districts like Singalong, San Andres Bukid, and Sampaloc, one searches in vain for growing churches. In the middle-class suburbs, on the other hand, one finds the typical Filipino Protestant church, "made up of the 'comfortables' and the better off common *tao*."[21]

In Madras, India, almost half of the 2.5 million people live under substandard conditions in the city's slum districts and on pavements. Amirtharaj Nelson describes them as "receptive peoples." But inside the 1,202 districts he designates as slums (*kudisai pakuthigal*) one finds not a single congregation of the Church of South India, the Methodist Church, or any other mainline denomination. In fact, during the years since Independence in 1947, the seventeen old, historic, wealthy churches of Madras have planted only six new congregations. "Some of these have been planted by accident, or by migration of members to new areas. These 17 churches have no intention of churching [metropolitan] Madras' three million," Nelson writes.[22]

Nothing changes as one moves into Europe and North America. Donald McGavran comments, "Anglicans, Lutherans, Presbyterians, Catholics in Europe have largely lost the working classes." An Anglican clergyman remarks to him, "After the industrial revolution started, we never had the working classes, and the Methodists got only a small part of them."[23]

There is a widening gap in Britain between the church and the workers in industry; the majority of the workers are outside the church. A trade union leader asks, "Have workers turned away from religion? If you asked them, I think you could be satisfied that most of them have accepted Christianity as a basis for their living. The real problem is that people do not see now that the churches and chapels are part and parcel of the struggle they are involved in." A retired official of an engineering union comments, "The language used in the Churches was often criticized as being 'mumbo-jumbo,' unintelligible and unattractive to the worker." Still another remarks, "People want something else besides material things, but they are not getting it from the very place where they should be able to get it."

The theme is repeated time and time again: the church is definitely out of touch with working-class people. A middle-aged man working on the factory floor in an automobile plant went to church. But in his congregation he was one of the very few people who were not white-collar workers, and he felt that some members of the congregation looked down on him. "The services were often above him. It was difficult to find a church which had a 'down-to-earth message relevant to everyday life.' "[24]

In the United States, we hear echoes of the same theme. Papers read at the 1980 Congress on Urban Ministry, sponsored by the Seminary Consortium on Urban Pastoral Education (SCUPE) and held in Chicago, repeat the message. "The mainline church has never really established itself among the city's poor and minority populations," says the director of Patchwork Central Ministries. The church in America is characterized by "its lack of commitment to the poor and its growing identification with middle-class success, affluence, and upward mobility," charges the director of the Urban Church Resource Center. A more recent study of the blue-collar worker and the church begins with this indictment: "It is my conviction that the church does not understand working-class people, and that ministry with working-class people is not a priority for most main-line denominations."[25]

How does one explain this gulf between the church and the poor and working classes of the world? There are several reasons.

Chief among them may be the identification of the church with the world's middle and upper classes. "In the United States, where all segments of the body politic are relatively affluent, many laboring men and women are Christians; but here, too, redemption and life make many congregations and denominations middle-class organisms and rather pleased at being such," writes Donald McGavran.[26] The missionaries the congregations send into the world's cities are middle-class people. The Philippines repeats the pattern. "This is the class of people that the average missionary understands best and feels at home with. Therefore, consciously or unconsciously, this is the class of Filipinos he has sought out."[27]

Related to this is a failure to develop an institutional lifestyle that communicates to the urban poor. The churches planted by middle-class missionaries or church leaders are middle-class in style. The biblical demand for "reverent worship" is transformed into a middle-class call for nineteenth-century, Western hymnody, an hour of silence during which only the preacher speaks, and the absence of African drums or Mexican guitars. The structuring of church government is dominated by a search for efficient ways of conducting business. Theological training schools call for more "quality education" for church leadership. But unwittingly, the process of academic training continues to abstract the leaders from their social setting and move them into the middle class.

Another related factor is the wider life of the church that often blocks the gospel in its passage to the poor and working class. One national group, quoted in a report at the 1980 Pattaya Consultation on World Evangelization, said,

> Within ourselves we discover an unwillingness to accept fully the pattern of the Incarnation. Even when we set out to work with the urban poor, we find that our institutions are organizations that actually shield us from the painful realities of poverty and divide us from those who are poor.[28]

The long-established gulf between the church and the marginalized removes spiritual expectancy; a fatalistic resignation immobilizes effort and prayer. This is reinforced by Christian evasion of corporate sins such as racism and social injustice.

There is also insensitivity to the steady social process of upward mobility. Even churches planted among the poor and working classes, through that process, shift into a middle-class pattern. The older the church in Africa, Asia, or Latin America, the more middle-class are its controlling members, provided it has used Western models for its maturing. McGavran notes,

> Not everyone becomes educated and middle-class, but those who do, control the Church. They are the ministers, elders, deacons, church school teachers, and heavy givers. The smaller the number of communicants in relation to the mission resources, the more rapidly does a Church become middle-class.[29]

There is increasing reason to believe this problem is appearing in the Korean churches. Originally associated by deliberate missionary design with the common people in a feudalistic culture, the church has found itself more and more identified with the middle class. Though Korea's cities are dotted with churches, the buildings the church members erect take on more and more the look of affluency and wealth. The congregations now face the serious danger of alienation from the urban poor, who may find little in common with them in the years just ahead. They will be seen increasingly as middle-class oriented and indifferent to involvement in political and cultural action for social change.

COURSE CORRECTIONS

Can this picture of urban conflict between the powerful and the powerless be changed? Has it been painted with total accuracy? Are there any modifications to the generalizations we have made? Are there—can there be—churches in which the poor and the working class feel at home?

1. *God can reorient urban power structures.* Some sense a deep fatalism in the proverbs that emerge from our view of cities. "What can you do?" "It's all too big, too overwhelming." "You can't fight city hall." All these at first sound tinged with a despair that borders on hopelessness.

But God's perspective reminds us that patterns can be reversed. Sovereign grace is large enough to shift even the weight of great cities. Nineveh in the eighth century B.C. had "more than a hundred and twenty thousand persons who do not know their right hand from their left" (Jonah 4:11). Despite the smug prejudice, empty traditionalism, and exclusive "stonewalling" of Jonah, the word of his Lord could bring the whole city to faith in God (3:5).

Those who possess power do yield to divine nudging. A fifty-five-year reign—a trail of power highlighted by pride, child sacrifice, and syncretistic animism—ended with repentant Manasseh restored (2 Chron. 33:1–13). Nebuchadnezzar, who boasted of "Babylon the great" built by his own hand for the glory of his majesty (Dan. 4:30), turned from self-praise to "exalt and honor the King of heaven" (4:37). Ephesus, the most important city in the Roman province of Asia, was shaken by a movement to Christ among the religious power brokers. "A number of them who had practiced magic collected their books and made a bonfire of them in public. The value of these was calculated to be fifty thousand silver pieces" (Acts 19:19, JB). The powerful in the world of animism discarded the secret names with secret authority in order to magnify another power name, the Lord Jesus (Acts 19:17).

The subsequent history of the church is dotted with similar points and periods of renewal. They come clustered around such common features as dependent prayer, a new sense of community, revitalized theological reflection, and disengagement from worldliness. And always, notes Richard Lovelace, they come associated with a new sense of mission—word and deed, evangelism and social concern for the poor.[30]

Geneva in the sixteenth century was "a crowded, bustling

commercial town, bursting at its walls."[31] Like all cities, it had its haves and its have-nots. It was a city of perhaps 10,300 by mid-century, but its population very likely doubled within a decade as impoverished refugees fled persecution in France and elsewhere in Europe. Inflation was eating away the economy of the city and, as always, hitting the poorest the hardest.

Under the direction of a French immigrant, John Calvin, the Bible was rediscovered, and its vitality touched church and society. Calvin read the words of his Lord in 2 Corinthians 8:13 recommending a new apportionment of wealth "that we may, in so far as every one's resources admit, afford help to the needy, so that there may not be some in affluence, and others in need." The 1559 edition of his *Institutes of the Christian Religion* summarizes his sense of obligation to the urban poor: "the church has gold not to keep but to pay out, and to relieve distress. What need to keep what helps not? . . . 'Whatever, then, the church has was for the support of the needy'" (IV.iv.8).

In that spirit Calvin struck down the ancient practice of usury, condemning the taking of interest when lending to the poor. He rediscovered the role of deacon as ministering to the poor. One-third of the city's revenue from fines went to that diaconal work and one-third to the poor of the city. To halt inflation, the wages of the city's employees were voluntarily lowered from 125 florins to 100 and then to 50. "So these magistrates decided to start where few politicians today would even think of beginning—with their own salaries."[32]

Public works programs were initiated to employ the refugee and the poor. In 1545 the city council, with Calvin's support, "ordered that they should be put to work for the city, each according to his ability." The refugees and the poverty-stricken were employed to construct the ramparts of the city. In the spring of 1554 four hundred families were put to work digging ditches, being paid by the job, not the day, so that they could work as much or as little as they wanted. This aspect of the Reformation demonstrated a built-in denial of urban despair; the marginalized, the underbelly of the city, learned again an old lesson: the pursuit of God leads not to profit, but to the poor.

The lesson was taught again in eighteenth-century England. John Wesley's ministry made one of its greatest contributions in recapturing the alienated poor for the church. Michael Paget-Wilkes describes what happened:

> Here was a religious movement that truly affected and converted the working class man, even in the depths of his misery. Methodism had a great following in the working class, in the industrial cities, and influenced even the radical thinkers. Wesley's preaching had a profound influence. The class meetings, and the community spirit that developed within them, enabled the movement to grow impressively, and the working man to grow in self-confidence. The movement showed that working men could organize themselves, and that leaders could emerge from their midst. Christianity was seen to be concerned about a human being's physical welfare and men taught that God hated the evils of exploitation.[33]

The England of Wesley's day was still largely rural. But industrialization had begun to change that by the latter half of the eighteenth century. By 1800, nine years after Wesley's death, England and Wales were 21 percent urban, and that percentage doubled in the next fifty years. The problems we now label "urban" were already apparent. People had begun to pour into the cities to work in the expanding mills and factories. A new class, the laboring class, was forming as a necessary adjunct to the machine. And beneath this group was the great mass of poor, making up half of the population at the beginning of the nineteenth century.[34]

When there was a shortage of adult male labor, it was made up by children and women. Factories seemed like prisonhouses. Sixteen-hour days were not exceptional. "The factory worker belonged to the dispossessed. He enjoyed neither status or power. If the new industrialist was the most powerful economic figure ever to have arisen, the factory labourer, especially if a woman or a child, was the most powerless."[35] One-quarter of the national income was shared by only 3.5 percent of families. Three-fifths of the total population lived on one-sixth of the national income.

In its initial stages, the Wesleyan movement did not touch these problems. But it reached the working class with a new sense of self-worth. It was out to reform a nation, but this meant primarily, almost exclusively, the individual citizen. Meanwhile, Methodism also attracted the new "bourgeoisie" of the day; the "captains" of industry were frequently among the leading evangelicals of the day and were to some extent responsible for the tragic conditions of the laboring poor. It was, in fact, more a religion *for* the poor than a religion *of* the poor. "There was," argues one critic, "little insight into the way in which social practices enter into and affect what we are and what we do."[36] "Systemic injustice," the subject of our discussion in an earlier chapter, was largely unrecognized at this point.

This was to change. The evangelical renewal began to touch the power wielders. Clapham Commons, a village three miles from London, was home to a wealthy group of evangelicals. And these men, dubbed the Clapham Sect by their foes in Parliament, provided a broad, popular base for radical social achievements into the nineteenth century. William Wilberforce led the battle in Parliament against slavery and lived to see the abolition of the slave trade (1807) and then slavery itself (1833) in the British Isles. A boycott of slave-produced goods was part of that campaign. Granville Sharp was chiefly responsible for the founding of Sierra Leone for freed slaves in 1787.

Other lives touched by sovereign grace reached out to touch society. John Howard, described by Wesley in his *Journal* as one of Europe's "greatest men," spent thirty thousand pounds of his own money and traveled fifty thousand miles in his effort to bring about prison reform in England and continental Europe. Michael Sadler, an evangelical Anglican, was the leader of the factory reform movement, and his work was carried on by Anthony Ashley Cooper, the seventh Earl of Shaftesbury.

Under Shaftesbury's influence, England's first child labor laws were enacted. The ten-hour day and the fifty-eight-hour week became law in 1848. In 1875 his legislation put an end to using preteen children as chimney sweeps. At the urging of Florence Nightingale, a Sanitary Commission sponsored by Shaftesbury set out in 1855 to study conditions in hospitals in the Crimea. The commission, according to Nightingale, "saved the British army." Shaftesbury's family motto exemplified his evangelical concern: "Love, Serve."[37]

2. Evil and powerlessness are not strictly urban problems. For the average person on an American street, to speak of cities is to speak of disorientation and marginalization. The picture that forms is one of despair, squalor, and immobility in the face of an invisible system of power to which the urbanite has little access. "Overurbanization" is a disaster, creating a parasitic people in the urban social system. The poor are seen as victims of the city. Many of the testimonies and data cited in the earlier part of this chapter ring with this kind of language.

Taxi Driver, a 1976 film, portrays this picture of the city. It is a two-character study—Travis, the taxi driver, versus New York. As interpreted by the director, the city is hell. There's no grace, no compassion on the street. The neon reds, the vapors that shoot up from the city gratings, the dilapidation all press in on the driver and on us. The city's filth and smut obsess him. "He is desperately sick, but he's the only one who tries to save a twelve-and-a-half-year-old hooker, Iris (Jodie Foster); the argument he invokes is that she belongs with her family and in school—the secure values from his own past that are of no help to him now."[38] In the end, violence is Travis's only means to express himself. When he does, he becomes the city's hero. The city has become crazier than he is.

Early theories in academic urban studies reiterated these connections between powerlessness and the city. Attention focused sharply on the question of marginalization as a characteristic of the poor. The underside of the city, skid row residents, prostitutes, and street gangs received extensive treatment in the literature.

Contemporary studies are correcting these directions in many ways. Embodied in the older studies, it is recognized, is a failure to see the city as a whole. Anthropology was only *in* the city, not yet *of* the city. The city was the background for study; it had not yet truly become the object of study.[39]

Increasingly also, as we have seen, studies have called into question such dichotomies as rural and urban, power and power-lessness. At best, such two-term classifications are heuristic perceptions of the ends of a wide-ranging continuum.[40] For example, it is true that large and dense populations are often poor ones. But cities also often have or have had the rich as well. Neither is marginalization by any means only urban. The migrant into the city was not necessarily powerful in the country or small village, only to become poor and disenfranchised in the city.

The Christian church has caught on very slowly to these corrections. Surprisingly enough, the Social Gospel movement, often popularly identified as the advocate for the urban, powerless poor, may be most guilty. To the promoters of the social gospel, the city was a moral peril. The growth of the large foreign populations in North American cities posed a threat to civilization. Samuel Loomis, citing population density in a way that Wirth did later, argued, "It was a comparatively small thing that the cities were vicious when they contained one-thirtieth of the people, but now they contain nearly one-fourth; soon it will be one-third, one-half; such fever-sores must not be ignored."[41] Riddled by a rural bias, social gospel advocates like Daniel Dorchester pointed the finger of blame for the city's deterioration at the immigrant poor.

> Our rural districts send valuable additions of virtue, intelligence, enterprise and real stamina; but other classes of a very different type pour into the cities—uneasy, restless, roving adventurers, needy and greedy men and women, thriftless families, many weary of the sweat of honest toil.[42]

Josiah Strong made it clear that the Protestant concern for the cities was based not on an affinity for urbanism, but on the ethnocentric argument that the cities were a vicious, dark source of eminent evils that spelled peril for Anglo-Saxon civilization: "The city has become a serious menace to our civilization, because in it, excepting Mormonism, each of the dangers we have discussed is enhanced, and all are focalized. It has a peculiar attraction for the immigrant."[43]

Given such a mentality, the reform efforts of the Social Gospel movement were directed toward neutralizing the perceived danger of the alien poor and the city as their shelter.

> The settlement houses and institutional churches were proposed and inaugurated as devices for subduing the foreign menace. The great wave of philanthropic effort . . . was not directed at concrete economic problems of unemployment and subsistence wages, but at evoking acceptable moral values and behaviour patterns among impoverished immigrants.[44]

The movement was a sophisticated effort at "blaming the victims"—the city and the poor. In the process, the real oppressors—ethnocentrism and prejudice—escaped under a cloud of ideological smoke.

3. Marginalization does not always mean powerlessness. The social gospel sank under the weight of its WASP mentality. But that same set of eyeglasses may still be hindering us in another way. Ethnocentrism and class bias still affect the way we see poverty as a hopeless, powerless lifestyle.

Recent studies urge us to look again. Marginality can become a stereotype, an ideological myth that inaccurately symbolizes weakness, frailty, and fatalism.

Janice Perlman lived in three of Rio de Janeiro's three hundred slums (*favelas*) for a year. Out of her interviews with 250 people, she saw the shanty towns of more than one million residents in a new light.

From outside, the typical favela seems a filthy, congested human antheap. Women walk back and forth with huge metal cans of water on their heads or cluster at the communal water supply washing clothes. Men hang around the local bars chatting or playing cards, seemingly with nothing better to do. Naked children play in the dirt and mud. The houses look precarious at best, thrown together out of discarded scraps. Open sewers create a terrible stench, especially on hot, still days. Dust and dirt fly everywhere on windy days; and mud cascades down past the huts on rainy ones.[45]

But to the insider, the picture is different. There is a remarkable degree of social cohesion and mutual trust. Oscar Lewis saw the members of the culture of poverty as removed and alienated, uninvolved and apathetic. An overall pessimism was said to paralyze action. But Perlman found that more than two-thirds of those she interviewed felt their lives had improved in the past and were going to improve in the future. And when the *favelas* suggest to us that "the poor don't have a chance," they are not reflecting inborn resignation and fatalism so much as a realistic assessment of their situation. The misery is real. But equally real is a pervasive optimism.

Neighborhoods seethe with movement. Workers chase over-crowded buses, women buy and sell in impoverished markets, children of every size still run and still play. There is construction everywhere. "Young people, an urban first generation, study and work and throw their energies into team sports, church groups and social action."[46]

"Sunrise in the Slums" is the title for a *Newsweek* article on these slums of Latin America.

In the midst of the pervasive squalor and crime there is often a curious sort of vitality. It may stem in part from sheer will to survive; many of the shanty towns throughout Latin America have successfully fended off attempts to clear them away, and have even organized themselves to become a powerful force in local politics. Moreover, slums in many countries are a primary locus of the *sector informal,* the vast

underground portion of local economies; the "informal" economic activity in the slums around Lima, for example, constitutes an estimated one-half of that city's total output. . . . The
slums are thus a genuine enterprise zone for many residents—
affording them the opportunity to scale part way up the
economic ladder, one shaky rung at a time.[47]

Why then are the slums pictured as places of powerlessness,
when someone like Perlman can describe their inhabitants as
possessing "the aspirations of the bourgeoisie, the perseverance of
pioneers, and the value of patriots"? The answer, says Perlman,
lies in middle-class and upper-class bias. "On the most fundamental level, the myths thrive not because of snobbery, moralizing, or
ethnocentrism, but because they fulfill the ideological-political
function of preserving the social order which generated them."[48]

The attitudes of people in the dominant groups thus tend to
be negative and pejorative whatever their political or ideological
persuasion. The paternalists emphasize the incapacity of the poor
by declaring that they can do no better. The liberals believe that
with their help the poor can better themselves and succeed in
attaining some of the values that the liberals also hold. The
radicals, though opposing the existing standards as they see them,
similarly expect the poor to accept their interpretation of the
changes necessary. No group favors independent action or wishes
to recognize the power of the marginalized. This would then
threaten either the existing structure of society or the superior role
taken by the observer.[49]

Sadly, the Christian community is not free of this same
perspective. Believers who are part of the middle or upper class
seldom reach below "their level" to plant churches among the
poor. Missionaries from outside the setting, unless they themselves have come from the slums, may emotionally contrast the
squalor of the slums with an image of idyllic rural life or suburban
comfort. They too find it difficult to see the slums as anything
except impossible. Plans for church planting seldom are directed
specifically at the slums. Executives wonder, "Will we find church

leadership there?" or "Is there enough financial viability to make a go of it?" The myth of marginality may play a deeper part in these questions than we care to admit.

In the frontier life of the United States in the nineteenth century, one finds remarkable echoes of this same vitality and struggle. Great growth took place among those churches that did not hesitate to move westward as the United States expanded. Methodist circuit riders and Baptist evangelists borrowed saloons for Sunday worship and adapted to the rough–and–tumble world of the frontier. The size of their churches today testifies to the wisdom of their choices. Can we become so depressed by the misery of the world's shanty towns of tin and reed mats that we cannot see there a dynamism to be harnessed for the Lord's service and enlarging opportunities for church growth? One of Donald McGavran's greatest contributions to missions has been his optimism. We must not lose it to the myth of marginalization.

4. Not all the churches have rejected the poor. The history of the Pentecostal churches in Latin America is a powerful reminder that there are churches in which the poor and working class feel at home. There the main growth of these congregations has been among the lower classes. In Chile, the Pentecostal churches have maintained an annual average growth rate of 6.5 percent since before 1930. They are the "churches of the laboring masses." What is their secret?

One group of observers suggests that "they deliberately concentrate on winning the lower classes, saying that these are the people who have proved to be winnable and that therefore it would be a mistake to try to win other classes."[50] A Chilean Pentecostal puts it this way:

> The other churches are trying to win the upper classes. If it is possible to win these classes, let the other churches win them, as they do not appear winnable to us. We do not want to cut ourselves off from the people we know are winnable and whom we are bringing to Christian faith.

In Nezahualcoyotl, Mexico, three million people live on a dry lake bed in a city that didn't even exist until the 1960s. Neza's first residents were mostly down-and-outers as poor, rural migrants erected their shacks there. In the process of becoming a middle-class city (the tendency of many shanty towns), Neza is in transition. And the evangelical churches have reached out to claim the city for Christ. Now there are at least 150 congregations in the city, with a worshiping community of fifteen to twenty thousand. The majority of these churches are Pentecostal-oriented fellowships.

An exact picture of the scene worldwide is hard to draw. Statistical information is not usually kept by denominations in terms of how many Christians are in the cities or how large (or small) is the income of those Christians. We are severely hampered in dealing with this issue by the church's traditional ignorance and lack of concern over societal and class realities.

This situation has begun to change recently, however. On the basis of his massive research in church demographics, David Barrett, the editor of the *World Christian Encyclopedia,* has outlined a sketch of "the church of the poor" on a worldwide scale. Global Christianity, he asserts, has become overwhelmingly the church of the rich. Average income at the world level is around $2,400 per person each year. He states,

> Because Christians are concentrated in the Western world, their average income . . . is far higher at $4,500. Non-Christians average only $1,350. . . . Since lifestyle depends on income, Christians across the world can be seen to live on average at a level over three times higher than non-Christians.[51]

Averages, however, do not tell the whole story. Income distribution is so unequal that, whereas 52 percent of all Christians live in affluence and a further 35 percent are comparatively well off, 13 percent live in absolute poverty. As defined by the World Bank, that term represents "a condition of life so characterized by malnutrition, illiteracy and disease as to be beneath any reasonable definition of human decency."[52] Over against a worldwide average annual income of $2,400, some 800 million people live on an income of less than $90 per year. And out of that figure, 24 percent—195 million—are professing Christians. Worldwide, that means that 13.4 percent of all Christians in the world live in absolute poverty. Of these, half live in Latin America, a third in Africa, the rest in South and Southeast Asia.

There is no room for triumphalism at this stage in affirming that not all the poor have rejected the church. It is denied by the reality that 750 million affluent Christians can continue to allow 195 million brothers and sisters in Christ to exist in abject poverty year after year. It is denied by the reality that

> in the actual denominations to which the 195 million belong, they exist in close proximity to some 20 million relatively affluent co-citizen, elite, fellow Christians above them. These include the hierarchies of church leaders who control the churches, few of whom are poor and a number of whom have become very rich since taking office. Regrettably, these 20 million show less concern for the poor than many of their co-religionists in the Western world.[53]

Can this picture be reversed? Are new models for the church emerging to challenge the status quo mentality of the Christian elite? We have mentioned the growth of the Latin American Pentecostal churches among the poor. What lessons do they offer us?

Some question just how deeply attached the Pentecostals are to the lower or working classes and how really radical they are in their challenge to the social structures of power. Mainline Pentecostals are said to have a middle-class orientation.

However, Guillermo Cook, in his surveys of these communities in Brazil, is not so critical. He concurs in admitting the Pentecostals' neglect of the structural dimensions of social evil. On the other hand, they confront real social evils on a different—spiritual—plane. Their confrontation is not entirely an otherworldly escape mechanism.[54]

This, argues Cook, is more evident outside mainline Pente-
costalism and within the dissident Pentecostal communities.
Within these groups the original traditions of Brazilian Pentecostals are being carried out. Those traditions, in the beginnings of
the movement,

> had discovered the political radicality of the gospel which
> the traditional religiosity of every confession tried to ignore:
> that the saint is "a poor man who condemns riches and a
> dominated man who condemns domination." . . . More re-
> cently . . . mainline Pentecostalism has lost this "saintly"
> quality in its search for ecclesiastical acceptance.[55]

Cook goes on,

> But among the agents of the small sects, those that see
> themselves as "the poor and humble," even as compared to
> "those believers in the churches," the feeling of a holy war is
> alive, together with the hope of a final struggle that will recreate
> a social order without "the power of the mighty of this earth,"
> and continues to be stronger than the hope of a personal
> salvation.[56]

Cook's guess? Should the moment come when the subordinated
classes are given an opportunity to participate in the political
process of Brazil, we would see a massive involvement of grass-
roots Pentecostal communities. In communities formed in a social
environment "where Christ is stronger" (to use a Pentecostal
expression), where the hardships of the poor are daily experienced,
the leap from a radical faith commitment to Christ in one part of
life to political power in another would not be a large jump.

A much more active model has already arisen within the
Roman Catholic Church, the Base Ecclesial Communities (BECs).
In 1981 there were an estimated 80,000 BECs in Brazil alone.
Deeply rooted in a lay agenda, they draw their membership from
"the bottom of society" (hence, the label "base"). They are the
despised, dominated, suffering, faceless poor.

But they are not powerless. Meeting in community together,
each group searches for ways to understand who they are as the

people of God and how they may give witness to their membership in the kingdom of God in a society inhospitable to the weak
and poor.

A group of less than twenty meets in a district in Santiago,
Chile. Joseph G. Healey describes the scene:

> After the Scripture reading and initial discussion, they
> began reflecting in Spanish on the unjust working conditions in
> the nearby paper factory which employed over 5,000 people and
> provided the main source of livelihood for the whole area. . . .
> Several . . . members described their dilemma as factory
> workers: if they protested against the unfair employment
> practices and lack of worker benefits, they would get fired and
> their families would suffer. Yet, they didn't want to remain
> silent in the face of unjust labor structures and oppressive
> working conditions.[57]

In another part of the same city, thirty people assemble in a
very poor neighborhood. There is Bible study and then a time of
planning for the week ahead. The majority of heads of families in
the community have no steady, full-time jobs, due to the high rate
of unemployment. This base community has initiated fourteen
self-help projects in that neighborhood—for instance, soup kitch-
ens, literacy classes, and child care. Some of them need greater
support than they are receiving.

> Two new topics are raised for discussion: how to do
> something to stop the city from cutting off the water of those
> who could not pay their bills; and, whether or not the few who
> had regular jobs should run the risk of losing them by taking
> part in the demonstration being planned for the following
> Sunday by the base communities as a protest against unemploy-
> ment. They all wanted to be part of this movement even though
> it might lead to beatings and arrests, but those who were
> employed needed the help of the community to decide where
> their responsibility lay.[58]

The meeting ends with a time of prayer.

And so the communities go—what one author describes as
"seeds of a new society built on human dignity, community, a

new way of being church, and social relationships of justness and brotherhood." Community organization has brought the poor together in an instrument of solidarity against injustice and oppression. And all this in the name of the gospel.

Deficiencies are present—an exaggerated swing in the direction of the social and horizontal dimensions of the gospel; a missing emphasis on regeneration and conversion, not only in response to our social relations, but in recognition of humanity's ultimate accountability to a Creator God; some confusion over the place of divine revelation as the ultimate arbiter of our sociocultural contexts and problems.[59]

But recognizing even these, we must also recognize something else. In the BECs the poor demonstrate their belief in the power of the gospel to change society. Calvin's Geneva movement and the Wesleyan revival, by comparison, depended not on the poor, but on the wealthy, touched by the Lord, to initiate change. Also, through the BEC movement, the church is changing. Out of it a power axiom is being reaffirmed: where the poor lead the church, the church listens to the poor.

5. Real power comes not from ruling over, but from serving with, the poor. Power plays are urban games. From Nimrod to Nebuchadnezzar, the urban giants have exercised what Max Weber called "the prerogative to determine what happens and the coercive force to make others yield—even against their own will."[60] American blacks who speak of "the System" are describing more than social structures and organizational management. They speak of marginalization, oppression, push and shove, pressure. The world of the city becomes a hierarchical structure, with a few on the top and the masses on the bottom.

The Bible points us in a different direction. As Israel prepared to shift from its semi-nomadic life of wandering to life in the cities of the Promised Land, God guided that change in direction through Mosaic legislation.

> Justice for the cities of the earth was part of the mission of
> Israel (Ezek. 18:5–9), an end to oppression, bread to the
> hungry, clothing to the naked, the execution of true justice
> between man and man (cf. Prov. 11:4ff., 19; 12:10, 26–28). The
> pattern remains the same for the New Israel in its preparation
> for the Kingdom of heaven (Matt. 25:31-40). Faith without
> works remains dead (James 2:14–17).[61]

More specifically, those works of justice are to be oriented to
the poor. As the sovereign protector of the poor and the dispenser
of justice, the Lord defined urban power in terms of the protection
of the weak and helpless, the prohibition of oppressive power
directed against the poor.

Power wielders especially were to exemplify this pattern.
Judges in the theocracy of God were to show integrity in
performing their duties (Deut. 1:16–17). When the city-states of
the Ancient Near East oppressed the Israelites, the judges became
saviors of the marginalized throng. This was to be preeminently
true of the kings of Israel. And when their power was turned
against the poor, afflicting grief instead of relieving it, God spoke
in wrath. Amid empty promises of servant rule from Rehoboam,
through the counsel of foolish young men, the discipline of whips
gave way to the threat of scorpions (1 Kings 12:6–11). And God
answered oppression with schism, a house divided against itself.

In the royal oppression of the poor, Amos saw the rejection of
God (Amos 2:4–6). Definitions of power were borrowed from
pagan neighbors and exhibited their godless fruits: "violence and
highway robbery" (Ezek. 22:29), landgrabbing (Mic. 2:2; Isa. 5:8),
the enslavement of the little ones (Jer. 34:8–22), abuse of power
and perversion of justice (Isa. 10:1ff.; Jer. 22:13–17). And all this
meant only one thing to the Lord: "What do you mean by
crushing my people, by grinding the face of the poor?" (Isa. 3:15).

With the coming of the Messiah, God's day of deliverance for
the poor arrived (Ps. 22:26; Isa. 11:4). From a feeding trough in a
Bethlehem stable would come the beginning of God's great urban
society, God's Son marching through cities in triumph on donkeys

and not warhorses (Luke 19:28–38). At the beginning of His ministry, Jesus is tempted to grasp power through a shortcut offered by Satan (Matt. 4:8–10). At its climax, He embraces powerlessness through death on a cross and God highly exalts Him (Phil. 2:8–9). His messianic ministry is certified to John the Baptist through His identification with the poor—the blind receiving their sight, the lame walking, the leper finding cleansing, the deaf their hearing (Matt. 11:5). Harlots and publicans will enter His kingdom before Pharisees. At the wedding feast of the Lamb will sit "the poor and maimed and blind and lame" (Luke 14:21).

This same pattern of the powerful identifying with the powerless is to characterize Jesus' disciples. Social hierarchies are upset by the ethics of the kingdom of God. The first will be last, and the last first (Matt. 19:30). In response to the request for power from some of His disciples, Jesus reminds them that they are copying a style of leadership characterize of the world. "You know that among the pagans the rulers lord it over them, and their great men make their authority felt" (Matt. 20:25, JB). The kingdom style is the opposite: "Anyone who wants to be great among you must be your servant. And anyone who wants to be first among you must be your slave" (Matt. 20:26–27). Our kingdom obligations toward the urban poor must be dominated by our new obsession for God and our neighbor. And who is our neighbor? Anyone who is in need (Luke 11:29–37).

As office had little to do with the concept of a ruling class in the old Israel, so it is in the new. The titles selected by our Lord to describe ministry do not center on position, prestige, and power.

> It seems that Jesus and the writers of the New Testament deliberately avoided the existing variety of religious terms (such as priest, ruler, rabbi, master), which might denote a special and privileged class within the church marked by domination over others, and chose instead *diakonos* and *doulos,* thoroughly secular words for the menial tasks of a slave: washing the feet of guests, waiting at table, serving food and pouring wine.[62]

Apostles become servants (2 Cor. 6:4), Paul a deacon (Eph. 3:7; Col. 1:23, 25). Elders are not lords, but examples (1 Peter 5:3). The fruit of the Spirit is not push, drive, climb, grasp, and trample; it is serve, love, give, do justice.[63]

The rediscovery of the office of deacon in the sixteenth-century renewal of the church was not a haphazard coincidence. The office is an expression of the heart of understanding power in the kingdom of God—compassion for the poor, the gospel response to the bitterness of human need and injustice (Acts 6:1–7).

Martin Luther King, Jr., offers this summary:

> There is nothing wrong with power if it is used correct-ly. . . . What is needed is a realization that power without love is reckless and abusive and love without power is sentimental and anemic. Power at its best is love implementing the demands of justice, and justice at its best is power correcting everything that stands against love.[64]

Around the tables of the world's cities, we are called again to reach for the top by reaching for the towel.

NOTES

[1] Gideon Sjoberg, *The Preindustrial City* (New York: Macmillan/Free Press, 1960), pp. 34–35.

[2] Lewis Mumford, *The City in History* (New York: Harcourt, Brace, 1961), p. 36.

[3] Jacques Ellul, *The Meaning of the City* (Grand Rapids: Wm. B. Eerdmans, 1970), p. 21.

[4] Alejandro Portes and John Walton, *Urban Latin America: The Political Condition From Above and Below* (Austin: University of Texas Press, 1976), pp. 17–18.

[5] Wayne A. Cornelius and Robert V. Kemper, eds., *Metropolitan Latin America: The Challenge and the Response* (Beverly Hills: Sage Publications, 1978), p. 39.

[6] Alan Gilbert, ed., *Urbanization in Contemporary Latin America* (New York: John Wiley, 1982), p. 70.

[7] Portes and Walton, *Urban Latin America,* pp. 90, 93.

[8] Quoted in Benjamin Tonna, *A Gospel for the Cities* (Maryknoll, N.Y.: Orbis, 1982), p. 24.

[9] Joan Nelson, *Access to Power: Politics and the Urban Poor in Developing Nations* (Princeton: Princeton University Press, 1979), p. 345.

[10] Timothy Monsma, *An Urban Strategy for Africa* (Pasadena: William Carey Library, 1979), p. 88.

[11] Chinua Achebe, *A Man of the People* (London: Heinemann, 1966), p. 19. Cf. Kenneth Little, *Urbanization as a Social Process: An Essay on Movement and Change in Contemporary Africa* (London: Routledge and Kegan Paul, 1974), pp. 20–31.

[12] Leland D. Baldwin, *The American Quest for the City of God* (Macon, Ga.: Mercer University Press, 1981), p. 199.

[13] Robert J. McClory, *Racism in America* (Chicago: Fides/Claretian, 1981), p. 65.

[14] Jim Wallis, *Revive Us Again: A Sojourner's Story* (Nashville: Abingdon, 1983), p. 109.

[15] James E. Blackwell and Philip S. Hart, *Cities, Suburbs, and Blacks: A Study of Concerns, Distrust and Alienation* (Bayside, N.Y.: General Hall, 1982), pp. 105–7.

[16] David Claerbaut, *Urban Ministry* (Grand Rapids: Zondervan, 1983), p. 104.

[17] Howard P. Chudacoff, *The Evolution of American Urban Society* (Englewood Cliffs, N.J.: Prentice-Hall, 1985), p. 254.

[18] Verley Sangster, *Every Kid* (Denver: Young Life Urban Ministries, 1984), p. 87.

[19] Kuo-shan Tsai, "How to Reach the Industrial Workers in Taiwan," *Chinese Around the World* (June 1985): 5.

[20] Keith Hinton, *Growing Churches Singapore Style: Ministry in an Urban Context* (Singapore: OMF Books, 1985), p. 113.

[21] A. L. Tuggy and R. Oliver, *Seeing the Church in the Philippines* (Manila: OMF Publishers, 1972), p. 138.

[22] Amirtharaj Nelson, *A New Day in Madras* (South Pasadena: William Carey Library, 1975), pp. 158–59.

[23] Donald A. McGavran, *Understanding Church Growth*, rev. ed. (Grand Rapids: Wm. B. Eerdmans, 1980), p. 282.

[24] K. A. Busia, *Urban Churches in Britain* (London: Lutterworth, 1966), p. 93.

[25] Tex Sample, *Blue Collar Ministry* (Valley Forge: Judson Press, 1984), p. 5.

[26] McGavran, *Understanding Church Growth*, p. 282.

[27] Tuggy and Oliver, *Seeing the Church in the Philippines*, p. 138.

[28] *The Thailand Report on the Urban Poor,* Lausanne Occasional Papers, no. 22 (Wheaton, Ill.: Lausanne Committee for World Evangelization, 1980), p. 14.

[29] McGavran, *Understanding Church Growth,* p. 282.

[30] Richard F. Lovelace, *Dynamics of Spiritual Life: An Evangelical Theology of Renewal* (Downers Grove, Ill.: InterVarsity, 1979), pp. 145–46.

[31] W. Fred Graham, *The Constructive Revolutionary: John Calvin and His Socio-Economic Impact* (Richmond: John Knox, 1971), p. 30.

[32] Ibid., p. 109.

[33] Michael Paget-Wilkes, *Poverty, Revolution and the Church* (Exeter, Devon: Paternoster, 1981), p. 60.

[34] Ernest E. Best, *Religion and Society in Transition: The Church and Social Change in England, 1560–1850* (New York: Edwin Mellen, 1982), p. 105.

[35] Ibid., p. 116.

[36] Ibid., p. 160.

[37] A full description of the social impact of the eighteenth-century renewal movement will be found in Earle E. Cairns, *Saints and Sinners* (Chicago: Moody, 1960).

[38] Pauline Kael, *When the Lights Go Down* (New York: Rinehart and Winston, 1980), p. 132.

[39] Edwin Eames and Judith Goode, *Anthropology of the City* (Englewood Cliffs, N.J.: Prentice-Hall, 1977), pp. 31–33.

[40] Conrad Arensberg, "The Urban in Crosscultural Perspective," in *Urban Anthropology: Research Perspectives and Strategy,* ed. Elizabeth M. Eddy (Athens: University of Georgia Press, 1968), p. 8.

[41] Samuel Loomis, *Modern Cities and their Religious Problems* (New York: Baker and Taylor, 1887), p. 106.

[42] Daniel Dorchester, "The City as a Peril," in *National Perils and Opportunities* (New York: Baker and Taylor, 1887), p. 21.

[43] Josiah Strong, *Our Country* (New York: American Home Missionary Society, 1885), p. 129.

[44] Jerry L. Tucker, "Protestant Ideology and Urban Reform in the United States" (Unpublished Ph.D. diss., American University, 1972), p. 227.

[45] Janice Perlman, *The Myth of Marginality* (Berkeley: University of California Press, 1976), p. 13.

[46] "The Pioneers," *Latinamerica Press* 16, no. 34 (20 September 1984): 3.

[47] "Sunrise in the Slums," *Newsweek* (24 June 1985): 64.

48 Perlman, *The Myth of Marginality,* p. 246.

49 Peter Lloyd, *Slums of Hope? Shanty Towns of the Third World* (New York: Penguin, 1979), p. 49.

50 W. R. Read, V. M. Monterroso, and H. A. Johnson, *Latin American Church Growth* (Grand Rapids: Wm. B. Eerdmans, 1969), p. 234.

51 David B. Barrett, "Silver and Gold Have I None: Church of the Poor or Church of the Rich?" *International Bulletin of Missionary Research* 7, no. 4 (October 1983): 147.

52 Ibid., p. 146.

53 Ibid., p. 148.

54 William [Guillermo] Cook, "Grass Roots Communities and the 'Protestant Predicament,' " *Occasional Essays* 9, no. 2 (December 1982): 83.

55 Ibid., p. 84.

56 Carlos Brandão, *Os Deuses do Povo* (São Paulo: Edit. Brasilense, 1980), p. 259.

57 Joseph G. Healey, "Let the Basic Christian Communities Speak," *Missiology* 11, no. 1 (January 1983): 27.

58 Richard Shaull, *Heralds of a New Reformation* (Maryknoll, N.Y.: Orbis, 1984), p. 121.

59 William Cook, "Evangelical Reflections on the Church of the Poor," *Missiology* 11, no. 1 (January 1983): 51–53.

60 Anthony Campolo, Jr., *The Power Delusion* (Wheaton, Ill.: Victor, 1983), p. 11.

61 Harvie M. Conn, "Christ and the City," in *Discipling the City,* ed. Roger S. Greenway (Grand Rapids: Baker, 1979), p. 250.

62 David Watson, *I Believe in the Church* (Grand Rapids: Wm. B. Eerdmans, 1978), pp. 254–55.

63 Cheryl Forbes, *The Religion of Power* (Grand Rapids: Zondervan, 1983), p. 67.

64 Mennonite Central Committee, *Food and Hunger Notes,* no. 34 (November-December 1985): 1.

The Monoclass Generalization: "Nobody in the City But Poor Folks"

Chapter Seven

The Monoclass Generalization: "Nobody in the City But Poor Folks"

What do white North Americans see when they drive through the city? They see abandoned houses, boarded-up stores, and broken windows. And through their stereotypes, the city becomes another dirty word for one class, the poor.

The Third World they visit through TV news sends them the same message. Downtown Nairobi is beautiful with its tall buildings and flowering trees. But four miles from the downtown area, along the banks of the Mathare River, live some ten to twenty thousand urban squatters. The houses, crammed together, are built of mud and wattle with roofs of cardboard, flattened tin cans, and sheet metal. The roads are makeshift, garbage is piled high in open areas, and children play in the dust.

Much of the world's urban explosion leaves its debris in the shanty towns. In the 1960s these contained a quarter of the population of such cities as Manila and Djakarta, a third of Mexico City, a half of Ankara and Lima. City population often increases at twice the national growth rate. And in some states the shanty towns and slums expand at double the growth rate of the cities. By 1990 three-quarters of Lima's population may be living in shanty towns.[1]

In Mexico the shanty towns are called *Los Villas Miserias*— "Cities of the Miserable"; in Argentina, *Bandas de Miseria*. In the United States we speak of *ghettos*. All the terms have one thing in common—their negative connotation. And all of them are frequently translated "city."

The effect of this image is twofold. It can close our eyes not only to the needs of shanty towns but also to the other groups that fill the city. And the same insensitivity that keeps us from planning churches for the slums impedes our vision for reaching the elite, the working class, the soldier, and the politician. All disappear in a monoclass generalization that sees only the poor. The world church builds its own ghetto for middle-income converts.

SEARCHING FOR A NEW WAY OF SEEING CITIES

Within the last decade especially, the world evangelical community has begun to grapple with this monoclass stereotype of the city. It has started to ask, "What is God trying to accomplish by the urbanization of His world and the international-ization of our cities?"

This new interest was given fresh impetus in 1980 when the Lausanne Committee for World Evangelization held a Consulta-tion on World Evangelization (COWE) in Pattaya, Thailand. One of the many mini-consultations around which COWE was structured was "Reaching Large Cities." In the follow-up program to that gathering, strategy priorities were oriented to "world-class cities," cities of international significance with populations of at least a million people.

It was determined that urban evangelistic strategy must be "contextually congruent with the sociologically and structurally complex natures of world-class cities, and developed in the light of the churches' total urban mission."[2] The strategy was to avoid a high-gloss "here's how," solution-oriented, prepackaged program. The feeling was that such programs too often produce guilt by success images and perpetuate dependency on Western, imported white male experts.

In keeping with this focus on process and not program, eighty-six cities have hosted Lausanne-initiated consultations since 1981. Dr. Raymond Bakke, professor of ministry at Northern Baptist Theological Seminary, was appointed to coordinate and participate in the gatherings. As a result of his extensive travels, reports are beginning to circulate regarding the gatherings.[3]

Paralleling this new focus on the city is a growing emphasis on "people groups" as a strategy tool. Until now, unreached peoples were categorized primarily in political terms—all the people living within the borders of a particular country. Ethnic, linguistic, social, and cultural differences were blurred by broad designations. "Consequently," writes Samuel Wilson, "evangelistic efforts which met with some success with some peoples would totally miss the mark with others."[4]

Through the research of men like Donald McGavran and Peter Wagner, the concept of a "people group" has narrowed that focus. Evangelical scholarship has begun to recognize the importance of dividing the world's population by people groups rather than by political boundaries. Making use of sociological studies, mission strategists have thought in terms of a "significantly large sociological grouping of individuals who perceive themselves to have a common affinity for one another."[5] Individuals, it is said, develop cultural patterns in the groups in which they find a sense of identity. These patterns include ways of thinking and acting. Communication flows easily within such a group. Within the group, people learn which roles to play. They learn who is "us" and who is "them." A bonding takes place that creates a special identity.

Discussion still goes on among evangelicals over questions related to the idea of a "people group." As defined by Donald

McGavran, does it become too optimistic a tool and forget that the community it creates can have a demonic side as well as God-given authenticity? Is the recognition of peoplehood so exalted by methodology as to become ultimately and solely a beneficial principle?[6] Does it end up stressing the pluriformity of the church more than its catholicity? If the breaking down of barriers that separate people in the world is an essential part of the gospel, not merely a result of it, doesn't an overemphasis on "people groups" inhibit the expression of that gospel "oneness"?[7]

Whatever modifications are finally made, the general concept of a society forming people groups cannot be denied. And it is an immense aid in helping the church see beyond its own "group" to those still not reached. Most church congregations, we have seen already, have been severely limited in their outreach to one or a few people groups similar to themselves. Samuel Wilson suggests,

> One way out of this situation is to introduce the concepts of people groups in terms of groups that *are* being reached. . . . When the church is taught to see those she has been reaching, she may be able to overcome its blindness to those not being reached.[8]

What need to be underlined now are the links between unreached people groups and the evangelization of the city. The strategy of reaching cities is not accomplished by ignoring people groups, but by looking for them. The strategy of reaching unreached people groups is accomplished not by ignoring the city, but by adding it to our church-planting agenda. Roger Greenway writes,

> We need to realize that cities are not single, homogeneous units but are conglomerates of thousands of different groups, many of which require a specially designed missionary strategy. The unreached in the city must be sought out, identified, studied and described before effective mission strategies can be developed to evangelize them.[9]

The cities of our time are honeycombed with people group compartments often even less visible to the naked eye than in rural locations.

A number of factors can hinder us from putting the two entities of unreached people groups and urban evangelization together. Until recently, the people group idea has been used widely and popularly in terms of tribal or more ethnically limited cultures. So at the back of the *Unreached Peoples* series of books published annually since 1979, one finds some two hundred pages listing well over three thousand unreached peoples. They are indexed by group name, by receptivity, and by religion, language, and culture. Rarely are they distinguished by urban location, even in the special volume of 1982 that focuses on urban peoples. Thirty-five peoples are listed in that same volume as "very receptive" to the gospel. But less than five are clearly identified as urban groups.

Undoubtedly, those who have provided information on these groups have not thought of the effect of the city on gospel receptivity. And the listings, after all, are dependent on many sources for the data. But if we are to connect the city with unreached people groups, more attention will have to be given to the urban setting.

Another barrier to linking the city with unreached people groups was mentioned earlier in this book. The city, to the popular eye (and especially the North American), is perceived as a "melting pot." Its ethnic and socio-cultural differences are believed to slowly evaporate into a new homogeneity identified only as "urban."

Australia exemplifies that egalitarian myth in a unique way. The profile of the Australian personality is that of mateship. David Millikan explains,

> The popular vision is of a society where wealth is evenly distributed, class distinctions will not be tolerated, where democratic principles have a sturdy and honourable tradition and where a man is judged first as a bloke before his status, job

or office is taken into consideration. Recent studies have shown this is not an accurate assessment. Peter Dwyer's *How Lucky Are We?* (ACC Publications) or *Social Stratification* by R. A. Wild (Geo. Allen and Unwin) makes it clear that Australia is not the classless society of the nineteenth-century myth.[10]

Still, Australians cling to an egalitarian attitude that mocks the distinctions of class that do exist. And this may be due, some argue, less with the absence of class and more with the peculiar success of the working classes. "In contrast with the USA and the UK," writes Eugene Nida,

> the working classes were able to make their case, especially in periods of high labour cost. It was this capacity which forced their cause on the attention of Australia and thus assured the notably egalitarian quality of Australian life.[11]

Sadly, that working class is the least reached by the church in Australia. The egalitarian attitude it helped to build has become a mythical wall that the church cannot penetrate. Related to it may be the common belief that the rural areas of Australia are more religious than the cities. In truth, there is no significant difference. The national statistics showing that 18.8 percent of the population attends church regularly apply equally to the country and the cities.

How serious are these kinds of barriers to linking people groups and the city? In an urban society, argues Eugene Nida, church growth is more likely to follow geographical, occupational, and friendship lines than family ones.[12] By contrast, a face-to-face society is built on what some call "primary networks," connections of kin and tribe. You know the town drunkard by name; you are known as a part of your family or tribal network. Everybody knows you and you know everybody. In such societies the predominant pattern of church growth is along clan or family lines.

In Korea, for example, churches in small towns or villages often grow to the size of fifty to a hundred members. But then growth stops, often for some time. In analysis of these churches it is generally found that a church has grown to include almost all the members of one dominant family in the area. The congregation is made up largely of members from, say, the Park clan or the Chung clan. It is rare in such circumstances that any other equally important family in the village will enter the fellowship. Family networks can thus become both "the bridges of God" and "the barriers against God."

In the city, however, family networks are only one method of socialization among many. Personal relationships and a sense of belonging can be created out of a commonly shared residential territory (a neighborhood). You build relationships with the mechanic who lives next door, the barber down the street, your child's teacher in the house on the corner. Vocation can bring non-neighbors together. You socialize with your fellow factory workers, the teachers in the same school where you work, the woman selling apples in the stall next to yours in the market. The city spawns such networks in much larger array than the village and rural cultures. People create an identity from a plural set of groups.

Failure to see these groups in the city can send us looking down the wrong street. In our search through Singapore we may miss the "cosmopolite." This people group, spurred by the government's aggressive promotion of ethnic and linguistic integration, has created its own urban lifestyle. These people are progressive and pro-government, and they communicate in English. They have similar incomes, ideas, interests, and types of housing. Class consciousness is high and ethnic consciousness low. They join clubs and churches marked by these new values, regardless of race.[13]

If you assume a functional egalitarianism to be the trademark of a "melting pot" city, you will likely miss the cosmopolite. If you look for only ethnic distinctives, you will miss them too. Ethnicity is not the focus of their people group. In fact, English-speaking churches in Singapore are the most interethnic social institutions in the state.

Are there networks that should be examined more carefully than others? Raymond Bakke argues that the vocational network is the key to evangelism in the city. In a rural setting the ethnic and geographical networks are especially visible.

> If people ask *who* we are, we tell them who we are related to and where we live. In a city, however, ask ten people *who* they are and they will tell you *what* they do. "I'm a teacher, lawyer, secretary." That is not who they are, of course. That is what they do, but that *is* the primary identity of most urban people.[14]

Given this fact, pastors and evangelists should probably visit urban homes less than urban offices, markets, or factories. A parish mentality that defines the church's parameters of ministry in terms of geographical area surrounding the church building may not be nearly so significant as where the people in that parish area work. In addition, the parish by its very nature sees itself as a "come" structure rather than a "go" mission.

In the end, then, we blame the big, bad city for our failure to reach it. And in the meantime, the real problem is the socio-cultural shortsightedness of the church itself.

THE SHAPE OF URBAN SOCIAL NETWORKS AND THE CHURCH

The New Testament pictured the church as a community drawn from a wide spectrum of social networks. Scholars in the past have argued that the early Christians were of low social status, a movement of the poor and deprived, a monoclass captivity.

More recently that judgment is being corrected. The apostolic church had a cross section of networks. The extreme top and bottom of the Greco-Roman social scale are missing. We meet no landed aristocrats, no senators.

> But there is also no specific evidence of people who are destitute—such as the hired menials and dependent handwork-

ers; the poorest of the poor, peasants, agricultural slaves, and hired agricultural day laborers, are absent because of the urban setting of the Pauline groups. There may well have been members of the Pauline communities who lived at the subsistence level, but we hear nothing of them.[15]

The levels in between, however, are well represented. There are both slave owners and slaves (Eph. 6:5–9; Col. 3:22–4:1; Philemon); we find wealthy artisans and traders (1 Thess. 4:11–12): high in income, low in occupational prestige. Wealthy, independent women like Lydia of Philippi (Acts 16:14–15) and "a number of prominent Greek women" in Berea (Acts 17:12) joined the fellowship, departing from traditional patterns of female social roles through public prayer and prophecy in the congregation (1 Cor. 11:5; 14:33–36).

Christians were to be found in "the household of Caesar" (Phil. 4:22), freedpersons who virtually constituted the civil service of the empire. One author suggests that the great majority of the Thessalonian Christians were manual workers, whether skilled or unskilled (2 Thess. 3:6–13). Paul's advice to the Corinthian church regarding the collection for Jerusalem Christians seems to suggest the economy of small people, not destitute, but not commanding capital either. The collection is to be assembled little by little, week by week (1 Cor. 16:1–4).

Differences between these social networks often created problems in the church. At Corinth the wealthy apparently made the common table into a "private supper" (1 Cor. 11:21), leaving the haves drunk and the have-nots hungry. Those who have houses are blamed for humiliating those who do not (11:22). Some have suggested that the Corinthian debate over eating meat offered to idols (1 Cor. 8–10) may have had social overtones. The "strong" may also be relatively more powerful socially and economically than "the weak." In Greco-Roman culture, the poor in fact rarely ate meat; the occasions when they did tended to be cultic, whether public or private. For wealthy people, who could have meat as a regular item in their diet, there would have been far fewer religious associations and much less trouble for their consciences.[16]

Against this background of social friction, Paul's argument for the unity of the church at the Lord's Supper (1 Cor. 10:16–17; 11:18–19) has more than merely theological significance. It is a rebuke of the expectations of a hierarchical society and a call to egalitarian community. Paul does not demand that the social networks be eliminated. But they must be so transformed by the grace of Christ as not to deliberately leave some "in" and some "out of" the fellowship.

Further, for Paul, wealth offers an opportunity to share (2 Cor. 8:13–15), power an opportunity to serve, prestige a calling to humility. The church is to be a community in which ethnicity ("neither Jew nor Greek"), sexual roles ("neither male nor female"), and societal differences ("neither slave nor free") cease to be instruments for maintaining network boundaries. Rather, they offer opportunities to demonstrate to the world's culture that we "are all one in Christ Jesus" (Gal. 3:28).

This unique approach to social networking in the first century had a strongly evangelistic intention. The structuring of the life of the church was done with an eye toward how outsiders would perceive the Christians. Paul's appeal to artisans "to lead a quiet life, to mind your own business, and to work with your hands" (1 Thess. 4:11) has, as its purpose, "that your daily life may win the respect of outsiders" (4:12). The Corinthian Christians are urged to put no stumblingblock before "Jews and Greeks and God's assembly" (1 Cor. 10:32). The exercise of the gift of tongues in public assembly is to be restrained lest visiting unbelievers think the Christians insane (1 Cor. 14:23). Any practices judged as "disgraceful" by the Gentiles' standards must be curtailed (1 Cor. 11:4–6). Colossians 4:5 sums it up: "Behave wisely toward the outsiders, and cash in your opportunity."

Social networks have become more complex since the time of the New Testament. In the Greco-Roman world "the basis of the class system was birth and legal status rather than wealth. A senator might not be very rich but he was at the top of the social hierarchy and was secure in his status."[17] Today, in any given society a large number of variables affect social ranking (called "stratification"): power, occupational prestige, wealth, education, religious and ritual purity, family and ethnic-group position, and local-community status.[18]

None of these are uniquely urban qualities. But the city does add two characteristics to the process of stratification: (1) It makes the networks more visible. "Cities characteristically contain people with the *greatest* affluence, the *highest* prestige, and the *largest* measure of 'social clout,' while simultaneously being the home of the poorest, the least respected, and the most powerless people."[19] And (2) cities continually draw to them people of every social stratum. The cities are perceived as places where greater opportunity exists.

To complicate the picture even further, these variables do not all have the same weight. Further, the weight of each factor depends on who is doing the weighing and in which culture the weighing is being done. Scholars like W. Lloyd Warner, who published the study *Yankee City* in 1941, defined six social classes that have shaped sociological perceptions of American cities since that time. But his classification system has been questioned. Whether right or wrong, it is not easily transposed onto other sociocultural systems.

By contrast, in many societies of the Third World there seem to be basically only two urban levels—"the class and the masses."

Jamaica exemplifies the class-mass structure. The classes form less than 10 percent of the population. Separating them from the masses are many of the variables we cited earlier. By 1962 the economic gap was severe. The income of the upper-bracket clerks, teachers, ministers, and government workers ranged from $1,500 to $3,000 a year; that of the laborers, renters, and small cultivators ranged from $200 to $300 a year. Educational differences are extreme. "The masses have many illiterates, many who have only two to four years schooling, and a relative few who have had six to eight years. The classes are educated people, read newspapers, magazines, and books, and are cultured citizens of the world."[20]

A racial gap persists in Jamaica. The classes comprise those who have European and African blood in their veins; the more European the blood and the lighter the skin color, the higher the standing. The masses are made up of dark-skinned people, and they find it harder to get jobs and harder to move ahead beyond the color line.

Language also plays a role in stratification. The classes speak excellent English, while the masses speak Jamaican patois. All public functions are conducted in precise English, the only language that counts socially.

How does all this affect the church's mission? The church is largely identified with the "upper" class. To be Christian is to behave like the class. If the churches are to reach the masses, reorientation is required. According to Donald McGavran, "They must champion the causes of the masses. They must fight for educational opportunity for the masses. . . . We need missionaries with an active social conscience."[21]

Africa offers other complications. Urban social networks derive from a mixture of ethnic tribal roots, political power strains inherited from colonial days, and the effects of wealth and education. Some question the application of the class concept to Africa. Others see a three-tiered social structure emerging from these crisscrossing lines. But only two are said to emerge in the West African city: the elite—few in numbers but highly visible— and the urban employed.[22] For the elite, political power, wealth, and education define place. For the urban employed, tribal and vocational loyalties may be stronger. In effect, there are two sociocultural worlds in the West African city: the world of the elite and the literate as contrasted with the world of the urban worker.

The gospel will not penetrate the urban world of West Africa till these social networks are seen as pieces of the mosaic that makes up the city. The church in West Africa must continue its penetration of the rural masses, but new strategies and priorities are needed to reach the elite and the urban worker. That cannot happen if the African urban setting is defined only along lines of tribal affinities. The urban West African has other factors that play a part in self-definition: education, ambitions, and political loyalties. These too must play a role in reaching urban people groups with the healing touch of gospel hope.

The strategy planning of evangelicals has not always been sensitive to these factors. Even those concerned with the significance of people groups for evangelism are sometimes shortsighted. At the 1980 COWE gathering mentioned earlier in this chapter, there was a deep feeling among many of the eight hundred delegates that these dimensions had been neglected in the discussions. "A Statement of Concerns" was circulated and signed by nearly two hundred delegates, appealing for amplification of these issues.

In part, the Statement reads:

> Since the world is made up not just of people groups but of institutions and structures, the Lausanne Movement, if it is to make a lasting and profound evangelistic impact in the six continents of the world, must make a special effort to help Christians, local churches, denominations and mission agencies to identify not only people groups, but also the social, economic and political institutions that determine their lives and the structures behind them that hinder evangelism. Indeed, to be an effective mobilizing agent for the evangelization of the world, the LCWE (as the visible expression of the Lausanne Movement) will have to give guidelines to Christians in many parts of the world who are wrestling with the problems of racial, tribal and sexual discrimination, political imperialism, economic exploitation, and physical and psychological harassment of totalitarian regimes of whatever ideology (i.e., tortures, unjust imprisonment and forced exiles) and the liberation struggles that are the consequences of such violent aggression.[23]

The Statement, as I interpret it, is an effort not to divert the church from its evangelistic track, but simply to amplify the complexity of that task and the complexities that go into making up a people group. These complexities are intensified by the urbanization process and become all the more urgent in identifying and understanding the social networks that constitute the city's unique challenge. Vinay Samuel and Chris Sugden wrote hopefully, "The people group approach when applied not only to religions and cultures, but also to the socio-economic, political and ideological realities of life can help Christians relate the gospel to the whole life of the world."[24]

SOCIAL NETWORK EXAMPLES

1. The Elite, wherever they live and thrive, exist as islands of prosperity and power, a room at the top. Their lifestyle symbols speak of exclusivity—a swimming pool in Bel Air, California, or a private car in societies in which most people can barely afford a bicycle. Urbanization widens the gap between them and the masses, and even more so in Third World countries where there is not a strong middle class. Of this, Benjamin Tonna writes,

> The lifestyle of the well-off is characterized by a vivid concern for their own interests. Based in the city, they often have been educated in the West or along Western lines, and they know how to close ranks against the "threats" of competitors, taking political power into their own hands. They know, further, how to close ranks against all the others; rarely do they marry outside their own circles, and they keep to themselves as to schools, residential areas, and social outreach. To this aim they tend to display, rather than camouflage, their affluent lifestyle.[25]

Every country and every city have some elite—perhaps 1 percent in Upper Volta, 5 percent in Kenya, 20 percent (almost all white) in South Africa, 4 percent in Brazil. Their numbers are few, but their status and influence are great.

In Africa, several features distinguish the urban elite. Unlike the rural elite, where age is the principal determinant of status, they are comparatively young, often in their thirties and forties.

They tend to obtain their high position on the basis of achievement in addition to (or instead of) tribal connection. But their tribal roots are not forgotten. Nepotism is a charge frequently heard in the city. And for the urban elite, a co-ethnic political base makes cultivated attachment to kin an important part of the quest for power.

The African urban elite also tend to be employed in occupations that developed as the result of European colonization. They are school teachers, government administrators, and senior civil servants. And increasingly since the 1960s, they are the officer corps of the army and, to a lesser extent, of the police.

Unlike their rural counterparts, the urban elite are characterized by great specialization. In the towns there are key businessmen, lawyers, and bankers. This specialization is increasing.[26] Economic wealth is not always the determining factor in creating an elite base.

Though self-interested and isolated from the masses, they set the social pattern in everything from dress style to currently acceptable ideas and opinions. Through their knowledge of the colonial language, they know the world situation and naturally fill the leadership roles in the city and the country. Their influence extends far out of proportion to their small numbers. Though isolated by status, they are respected and copied by the community.[27]

In the United States the elite have spawned a new subgroup, the Yuppies (Young Urban Professionals). Like the African elite, they are young, between the ages of twenty-five and thirty-nine. Likewise, they reach their goals by achievement rather than connections. "Work hard, play hard" seems to be their motto.[28] They put in sixty-hour weeks at jobs in law, high technology, and business administration. They even "use leisure as a vehicle for corporate advancement," says one commentator. Often Yuppies gather at fitness spas for "business contacts," not for health benefits.

Unlike their African counterparts among the new urban elite, the Yuppies' lifestyle shows little directed orientation to the power of the political world. They appear distrustful of government and institutions—or perhaps anyone or anything that may demand community responsibility. One Yuppie T-shirt reads: NUCLEAR WAR? WHAT ABOUT MY CAREER?

The Yuppies are oriented around wealth and its personal use. Their average income is $40,000 or more a year. And there are apparently at least four million Yuppies who qualify economically for the title. The managing editor of *Money* summed up his magazine's conclusion that wealth has become their main obsession. "Money has become the new sex," he concluded. Laurie Gilbert, one frank Yuppie quoted in a *Newsweek* cover article, confessed to reporters that she would be "comfortable with $200,000 a year." The Yuppie, the *Newsweek* article continued, has achieved a new plane of consciousness: Transcendental Acquisition. Conspicuous Production for the Yuppie is wedded to Conspicuous Consumption.

The name of the game "is *the best*—buying it, owning it, using it, eating it, wearing it, growing it, cooking it, driving it, doing whatever with it."[29] Yuppies regard luxuries as necessities, finding it difficult to reach outside themselves. They give themselves gifts ("You owe it to yourself," the ads tell them). Cigarette advertisers appeal to them with slogans like "the taste of success." A recent beer ad campaign features happy, successful Yuppie types, and the soundtrack sums up the lifestyle: "You can have it all."

Can one reach these urban elite in Africa and in the "silicon valley" of the United States? Very few apparently have tried with a gospel word that makes divine demands of our world's rich young rulers. "You shall have treasure in heaven" does not appeal to elitist expectations. The price tag may be too high to pay, even for a Yuppie: "Sell all that you possess and give it to the poor" (Luke 18:22). There is surely little hope for a high yield in this harvest field; it is still easier for a camel to go through the eye of a needle than for a Yuppie to enter the kingdom of God (Luke 18:25).

But it is also true that impossible missions become "possible with God" (Luke 18:27). A Beyers Naudé can speak loudly, though silenced by the ban. A White House assistant to the President, Charles Colson, can find a new kind of political power in prison with Jesus. A wealthy businessman like Arthur DeMoss, founder and owner of one of America's largest insurance companies, can turn luxurious lawn parties for his friends into rescue missions for the "up-and-outers."

It is Colson, in fact, who offers some tentative guidelines for reaching America's—and the world's—Yuppies.

> First, we need to help the yuppies discover they are on a blind path. We don't have to club them over the head with our Bibles—but we can challenge them to recapture their lost social idealism by unmasking the emptiness of a life that depends on money, power and prestige for its satisfaction.
>
> Second, we can encourage spokespersons whom yuppies will respect. I was asked recently by a leading Christian publication to name the outstanding young evangelical leaders under 40; it was one of the shortest lists I've ever compiled. The evangelical caste system tends to stifle articulate young spokespeople. . . .
>
> Third, there are apparently some churches attracting young urban professionals. . . . We need to learn from these churches ways in which local assemblies might reach out, ways in which they can bring in and help meet the unspoken needs of the yuppies.
>
> Fourth, since many yuppies appear to have little interest in the organized church, we need to reach them on their own turf. Home Bible studies, morning prayer breakfasts, and the powerful testimony of unadulterated friendship evangelism may well reach yuppies in the midst of their overscheduled lives. . . .
>
> Fifth, the way in which our case is presented has a powerful effect. Yuppies may not be willing to listen to a thundering denunciation of the evils of alcohol and tobacco, or watch some arm-waving Bible pounder on television. But a reasoned argument . . . on the evidence for the existence of God might quietly penetrate the yuppie armor.[30]

A few words of caution are necessary in planning this elitist evangelism. Christians, warns Colson, are not immune to the seduction of money, power, and prestige. The church has girded itself for battle before—only to discover that the enemy is within.

Africa's history is important to remember on this score. The leaders of the major churches have become almost as integral a part of the governing minority in black-ruled Africa as in white. Adrian Hastings explains,

> The senior clergy share in the standards and status symbols of the affluent society, just as they share in many of its possibilities of power: in both ways they are only too clearly marked off from the poor and the powerless. The gift of a Mercedes from president to archbishop is now an almost ritual feature of African life.[31]

The church's past has been full of cross-pollination. Will we produce again our own crop of elitist "Yuppies—young, urban pew-sitting professionals whose faith is but a notation on their resumés and whose ornate churches are but a reflection of their social status"?[32]

Should we aim for the elitist classes first, with the expectation that they in turn will win the lower classes or the masses? That, warns Donald McGavran, has seldom happened. Far from a new religion being accepted first by the class and then by the masses, it is usually the reverse. Later, as in the case of Christianity in the Roman Empire, the classes accepted it. McGavran states, "Higher religions make their entry into society from below upwards and the dominant minority [the classes] is either unaware of these new religious movements or . . . is hostile to them. . . . [In the Roman Empire] the philosophies appealed to the middle class. . . . Christianity appealed to the masses."[33]

2. *The Middle Class* in white North America comprises the majority of the population and sets general standards for the rest of the nation. From its ranks has come the vast bulk of America's

Christians. Its mentality has deeply shaped the standards and strategy of the church's understanding of its mission.

But in the Third World, the so-called lower class constitutes the majority, and it is the upper class and not the middle class that sets the standards. The middle class represents a small but growing band in the major social struggle between top and bottom. Increasing in size, it is forever trying to catch up. In Latin America, the middle class is uniquely a product of urbanization and owes its existence to commercial and industrial development.

"Today the middle class is strongest in the cities of Argentina, Uruguay, Chile, Costa Rica, Mexico, Venezuela, and Brazil."[34] And these are also the countries with the highest rates of urbanization and literacy. As the cities grow, the middle class will also grow.

Virtually ignored by social scientists, ethnographers, and church planters alike, the size of the Latin American middle class is still difficult to determine. A 1960 study estimated the average for all the continent at about 20 percent. But the range is from 8 percent in Venezuela to 50 percent in Uruguay.

Many of the Latin American middle class, in contrast to the Northern Hemisphere equivalent, work for the government. This is especially true in the national capitals. In Lima, white-collar government workers outnumber those in the private sector. In Rio de Janeiro, a 1966 sampling found that more than one-third of upper- and middle-class workers were employed in the city's public bureaucracy. Under these conditions it is not surprising that the Latin American middle class tend to be politically conservative, to side with those in power, and to support the status quo. They become the chief support base for military dictatorship and share a value system and lifestyle closely patterned after the elite and those of the upper class.

Other occupational groupings fill out the class—the entrepreneurs with a stake in private property and free enterprise, the growing number of skilled artisans in various trades. Upward social mobility enlarges the middle class as the lower classes press into new sectors.

The Latin American evangelical church climbs through this same social process.

> Through education, improved standards of living, a wider understanding of the world, and the redemptive effect of the gospel, they have moved up the social scale into the middle class. This social advance may occur in the first generation, or it may take longer enough that only the sons or grandsons of Evangelicals reach the middle class.[35]

Evangelical churches, by and large, have been planted among the lower classes. The middle class itself has not been a specific target of evangelical mission. Like Topsy, it has "just grow'd," and now it has "grow'd up."

Problems have come with this means of evangelical entrance into the middle class. Such churches frequently find themselves isolated both from others in the middle class and from the lower classes from which they came. Their Protestant views and their lifestyle cut them off sharply from traditional Latin American middle-class attitudes and religion. They feel withdrawn from their own class, living as a minority. And, as is the case with people groups formed in part by social mobility, their tendency is also "to lose touch with the very classes from which most of the members originally came."[36] The middle class, even the Christians among them, rarely look back or desire to move down. The result is isolation and barriers to church growth, an evangelical middle-class ghetto with a minority mentality.

Recently new models have emerged to break through these middle-class barriers. Direct evangelistic campaigns are being launched with the middle class specifically in mind. The work of the Christian and Missionary Alliance in Lima is one such example.

For the first half of the twentieth century, Alliance work in Peru was rural. In 1958, that policy was adjusted and a congregation was planted in Lima. By the late 1960s the congregation had peaked at 180 members. The old mansion it had occupied on a major street in one of the better middle-class sections of the city needed to be expanded so that it could seat up to 500. With the encouragement and expertise of an American businessman operating in Peru, the church eventually enlarged its plans and began construction on a building that would seat 1,000.

Coordinating with this event, missionary and church leadership resurrected the previously used approach of an evangelistic campaign. A fifteen-month campaign schedule, *Lima al Encuentro con Dios* (LED), was launched. By 1983, more than 35,000 decisions had been recorded. The mother church, now with more than 1,000 members, occupied a tenth of a city block. The first daughter church, begun with 36 members in 1975, had a building that seated 2,000 filled to capacity within eight years. The pattern continues, with daughter churches already establishing grand-daughter churches.

A number of basic principles, not particularly unique, have governed the movement: growth through evangelism; the development of a massive network of prayer cells; inspiring leadership; deep involvement and commitment to LED; follow-up training for new converts and emerging leaders. What may be most distinctive is its deliberate focus on the middle class.

LED had its genesis in a middle-class church in a middle-class section of Lima. The program was led by internationals and nationals from the middle class. It is funded by middle-class money. And perhaps related to all this, it has placed strong emphasis on visibility. As Fred H. Smith explains, LED churches

> are located where people can find them and they are located where people can see them. They are in heavily populated areas and on heavily travelled streets. We might add that all LED churches are attractive churches which draw attention. This is one key argument for investing funds in buildings that will serve as "drawing cards." The Latin, like his North American counterpart, likes to go to church in a "nice" setting. The mentality that all Protestant churches in Latin America need to be small, out of the way, and in the poorer sections of town has proven in many cases to be a detriment to church growth.[37]

A similar vision for the middle class in the world's cities has guided the planning of Mission to the World, the denominational agency of the Presbyterian Church in America. By the late 1970s, the fledgling board had determined to focus its evangelistic efforts on cities and on the growing middle classes in the cities. Feeling that a team approach is especially appropriate for urban ministry, it encourages missionary candidates to recruit teams for ministry together in such cities as Santiago, Quito, and Nairobi. Two teams are being formed now for church planting among the middle class located in the western part of Mexico City.

One team effort, originally focusing its work on the village and rural areas around Acapulco, has retooled with the encouragement of the board. Outreach is now directed primarily to the middle and upper classes. Although several of their ministries are among the poor, team member Richard Dye explains that the team feels

> particularly burdened to reach the middle (and some upper) class people. Probably more than ninety percent of the churches in 1970 were composed of poorer people. One could count on the fingers of both hands the total number of business and professional men in all the evangelical churches combined. Our experience has been that this class is particularly open at this time and has been responsive to the claims of Christ on their lives. . . .
>
> Another major reason for working among the middle class has been the raising up of Mexican leaders for our churches. There is so much more potential among the more educated, the harder worker, the one who has made a go of it in the world. They are becoming natural leaders in a much shorter time than we have seen before.[38]

Like the Alliance experience in Lima, the team in Acapulco has found that a prominent, public place is valuable for drawing the middle class into the church. They make wide use of conferences held in hotels about twice a year which focus on concerns of special interest to the middle class. "We have had 500-600 people out to hear about family problems, sex, drugs, etc.—

modern themes that attract people who would never go to a Protestant church, but will go hear a special talk on the family in a hotel," Dye writes.[39] These functions do not take the place of personal witnessing or home Bible studies, but rather complement them in preparing people to eventually attend church services on Sunday.

Another commonly shared experience has happily emerged from both these middle-class models. The poor have also heard the gospel. LED in Peru has seen many churches spontaneously springing up in the lower-class *barrios* of Lima, and a good percentage of those attending the two largest congregations are from the poorer classes of Lima's society. The Presbyterian work in Acapulco hopes and plans for the same to happen there. In fact, adds a team member, it has been gratifying already to see new middle-class believers reaching out to help the poor.

How widely this ripple effect will carry toward the poor remains to be seen. It flies in the face of past experience. Its force will depend on at least two factors: How seriously are kingdom obligations for the poor and oppressed going to be taught in the church and incorporated into the discipling follow-up for new middle-class believers? And how fully will the newly planted churches model these in their structures and program?

3. *The Refugees* are neither a uniquely urban nor a uniquely modern problem. In the Old Testament, their history is divinely woven into a paradigm of the lifestyle of the people of God. Abraham, the nomadic pilgrim finally driven by famine to Egypt, became a role model for the church as "an alien living in the land of promise, as in a foreign land" (Heb. 11:9). The oppression of the people of God in a foreign Egypt under a flinty Pharaoh culminated in an act of redemption whose vocabulary becomes standard New Testament language to describe the salvation Christ offers His pilgrim people (Rom. 3:24; Gal. 4:3). The exile that scattered the twelve tribes across the earth repeated the exodus pattern of salvation from Egypt (Ezek. 20:33). God will come

again to rebuild His refugee people and "make a way in the sea, a path in the mighty waters" (Isa. 43:2, 16, 19). And in Jesus, the "new Moses," the refugee from Egypt (Matt. 2:15), the ultimate exodus deliverance begins at Calvary (Luke 9:31). The disciples of Jesus become new "aliens and exiles" (1 Peter 2:11).

As aliens rescued by God, the Lord's people are to model compassion and justice for the other aliens living among them (Exod. 12:49; Deut. 1:16; 24:19, 21; 26:12–13; Mal. 3:5). The neighbors they are called to love as themselves are strangers in their midst (Lev. 19:18, 34). The calling is underlined in the New Testament (Matt. 19:19; Mark 12:31), where Samaritans become good neighbors (Luke 10:36–37) and the care of strangers is equated with care for Jesus and His people (Matt 25:31–46).

The last few decades of world history have intensified those images for many of us. The momentum of world politics, the complexities of famine and drought in Africa, and wars in Central America and Southeast Asia have left us faced with illegal aliens in Nairobi and Khartoum, applicants for asylum in Houston and Bangkok, economic and political refugees from Afghanistan. The geography of refugee flight includes Haiti and Cuba, Vietnam and Kampuchea, Ethiopia and Uganda. Every province of the Peoples Republic of China is now represented by refugees in a very small section of Chinatown in one city of the western United States.

How many refugees are there? If one includes those internally displaced within their country of origin and those already accepted for resettlement, the figure reaches 16 million worldwide. Without these qualifications, the number is 10 million.[40] The Middle East accounts for more than 4 million of them, with 2.6 million from Afghanistan alone, followed by more than 1.8 million Palestinians. There are 2,251,600 refugees from Africa.

These refugees come with scars formed in the land of their origins and in the countries that give them asylum. There is guilt over loved ones left behind, a sense of invulnerability radicalized by their survival, an aggressive willingness to take risks. In their host lands, they struggle with the trauma of radical culture shock, sharp changes in their social and economic status, and inhospitable neighbors who regard their presence as more competition for fewer jobs. Conflicts in the United States between blacks and Asians frequently reflect this economic struggle.[41]

Where do refugees settle? World refugee statistics for 1982 list at least seventy-seven countries that have offered refuge, many of the victims housed in refugee camps, processing centers, or villages that spring up almost overnight. Many will eventually end up in the world's larger cities.

One million Chileans have left their country since the military coup in 1973. Ten thousand have found their way to Canada, with the majority choosing to live in urban centers—Montreal, Vancouver, and Toronto. In the last decade, some 80,000 Soviet Jews have come to the United States, where nearly 43 percent have chosen to settle in New York City. Cuban refugees added 260,000 people to Miami in the 1960s, and today the city census lists at least 600,000. People now call Miami "a Latin American city." During the war in Southeast Asia, Michael Griffiths reports, "the population of the city of Phnom Penh increased from half a million to two million people; three out of every four were refugees. When the war ended, these people were all driven out into the countryside by force."[42]

Cities in the United States form a microcosm of the needs the refugees bring and the demographic pressures they create. Since 1970, the U.S. has taken in almost 4.4 million immigrants and refugees. More than 700,000 Indochinese alone poured into the U.S. during the past ten years. As many as 600,000 undocumented persons enter the country illegally each year.

By and large, within the church there is little or no awareness of these profound demographic shifts. Orlando Costas writes of the Hispanic community,

> Twenty-five years ago, there were some 5 million Hispanics in North America; by 1981, the official number was 15 million, with an unofficial estimate of more than 23 million. This translates to a growth rate of 2.2 percent per annum. The

sheer size of this ethnic bloc would seem reason for North American society in general, and the mainstream church in particular, to make Hispanics a top priority for the 1980s. But in point of fact, we observe no such interest. Instead, both the North American church and society at large appear uncon-cerned and uninformed about the Hispanic community.[43]

An exciting exception is the Southern Baptist Convention. Its members currently worship weekly in eighty-seven languages in more than 4,600 language-culture congregations. The Conven-tion's Language Missions Division has set a goal of reaching 3 percent (2.9 million) of the ethnics in the U.S. by the end of the century. To do that, it will expand its outreach to one hundred language groups by the end of the century.

But such goals remain the exception and not the rule in the United States and the rest of the world. Refugees are the focus in the 1983 edition of *Unreached Peoples*. Forty-three pages are devoted to "expanded descriptions" of forty-one refugee groups in almost as many countries. For each group there is what is called an "evangelism profile," indicating the approximate percentage of the group at various levels of awareness of the gospel. After every group appear the words "Not reported." The brief reports also carry a line to indicate the churches and missions working with the designated groups. Twenty-six groups bear the words "Not reported" after that category. Report after report speaks of needs and opportunities. Are they being met by the church? "Not reported" is the answer. Thus far the history of church planting among refugee and immigrant populations is an "if only" record.

Are there conclusions to be drawn from this look at refugees in the world's cities and, further, from our broader survey of the multiclass picture of the city? Borrowing from the language of Peter Wagner, with some modifications and expansions, we suggest that a faithful church needs to recognize at least these points:

a. The church needs to recognize that the gospel has spread

and will continue to spread most naturally in the city through people groups. The evangelistic task should be seen not so much in terms of individuals or countries as in terms of peoples.

b. The church needs to recognize that these people groups are formed in the city through various channels—ethnic, economic class, interests, vocations, neighborhoods. To isolate the evangelistic task from social, economic, and political issues is to minimize the cultural realities that go into shaping these groups. The whole gospel to be given to these groups will take more space than a file card can provide.

c. The church needs to recognize that in most cases each separate group will require churches of its own kind and style in order to develop and enjoy culturally and socially authentic expressions of Christian worship, community lifestyle, theology, ethics, and evangelism. People must be able to say, "God speaks my language." In the churches where that occurs, growth may often be fast and sure.

d. The church needs to recognize that merely declaring that "our church is open to all" is in itself a weak posture in a pluralistic society. Churches with "a little something for everyone" tend to be rather impotent community institutions. Aiming for everything usually hits nothing.

e. The church needs to recognize that structural racism can often subtly influence our desire to reach people groups. It can provide us with a convenient sociological tool for exclusion of others on the basis of race, ethnicity, or social class. In April 1985, a National Convocation on Evangelizing Ethnic America experienced something of the anger that can come from unintended planning mistakes in this matter. Limiting its scope to those groups whose primary language-culture identity was other than English, the convocation found itself facing a number of black leaders experiencing a sense of hurt that black Americans had not been included among the convocation's ten target groups. A convocation is now being planned to focus on black America.[44] But the pain will not be forgotten easily.

f. The church needs to recognize that the kingdom of God is much broader than congregations characterized by certain cultural identities. Over and above that, Christian people should take definite tangible steps to promote frequent in-depth contacts with Christians of other cultural groups. Only as this takes place and as strong bonds of mutual love and interdependence develop between Christians from diverse pieces of the city's cultural mosaic will the love of God pave the way for a national future free from the blights of racism, injustice, and discrimination.[45]

NOTES

[1] Peter Lloyd, *Slums of Hope? Shanty Towns of the Third World* (New York: Penguin, 1979), p. 20.

[2] Raymond Bakke, "Urban Evangelization: A Lausanne Strategy Since 1980," *International Bulletin of Missionary Research* 8, no. 4 (October 1984): 149.

[3] Raymond Bakke, "Strategy for Urban Mission," *TSF Bulletin* 8, no. 4 (March-April 1984): 20-21; Raymond Bakke, "Ministry in Large Cities Since Pattaya '80," in *The Future of World Evangelization: Unreached Peoples '84*, ed. Edward Dayton and Samuel Wilson (Monrovia, Calif.: MARC, 1984), pp. 121–30; "Evangelizing the World-Class Cities," *Together*, no. 2 (January-March 1984): 30–34.

[4] Samuel Wilson, "The Power and Problems of People Group Thinking in World Evangelization," in *Unreached Peoples '82*, ed. Edward Dayton and Samuel Wilson (Elgin, Ill.: David C. Cook, 1982), p. 20.

[5] Dayton and Wilson, *Unreached Peoples '82*, p. 7.

[6] Harvie M. Conn, "Looking for a Method: Backgrounds and Suggestions," in *Exploring Church Growth*, ed. Wilbert Shenk (Grand Rapids: Wm. B. Eerdmans, 1983), pp. 85–91.

[7] C. René Padilla, "The Unity of the Church and the Homogeneous Unit Principle," in Shenk, *Exploring Church Growth*, pp. 300–302.

[8] Samuel Wilson, "Power and Problems," p. 25.

[9] Roger S. Greenway, "Reaching the Unreached in the Cities," *Urban Mission* 2, no. 5 (May 1985): 3.

[10] David Millikan, *The Sunburnt Soul: Christianity in Search of an Australian Identity* (Homebush, N.S.W., Australia: Lancer Books, 1981), p. 18.

[11] Ibid., pp. 18–19.

[12] Eugene Nida, "Culture and Church Growth," in *Church Growth and Christian Mission,* ed. Donald McGavran (New York: Harper and Row, 1965), p. 95.

[13] Keith Hinton, *Growing Churches Singapore Style: Ministry in an Urban Context* (Singapore: OMF Books, 1985), pp. 78–79.

[14] Raymond Bakke, "Evangelization of the World's Cities," in *An Urban World: Churches Face the Future,* ed. Larry Rose and Kirk Hadaway (Nashville: Broadman, 1984), p. 86.

[15] Wayne A. Meeks, *The First Urban Christians: The Social World of the Apostle Paul* (New Haven: Yale University Press, 1983), p. 73.

[16] Gerd Theissen, "Die Starken und Schwaken in Korinth: Soziologische Analyse eines theologischen Streites," *Evangelische Theologie* 35 (1975): 272–89.

[17] Derek Tidball, *The Social Context of the New Testament* (Grand Rapids: Zondervan, 1984), p. 90.

[18] Meeks, *The First Urban Christians,* p. 54.

[19] James Spates and John Macionis, *The Sociology of Cities* (New York: St. Martin's, 1982), p. 361.

[20] Donald McGavran, *Church Growth in Jamaica* (Lucknow: Lucknow Publ. House, 1962), p. 27.

[21] Ibid., p. 31.

[22] Josef Gugler and William Flanagan, *Urbanization and Social Change in West Africa* (Cambridge: Cambridge University Press, 1981), p. 152.

[23] Orlando Costas, "Report on Thailand 80 (Consultation on World Evangelization)," *TSF Bulletin* 4, no. 1 (November 1980): 5.

[24] Vinay Samuel and Chris Sugden, "Let the Word Become Flesh!," *Third Way* 4, no. 8 (September 1980): 8.

[25] Benjamin Tonna, *A Gospel for the Cities* (Maryknoll, N.Y.: Orbis, 1982), p. 86.

[26] William Hanna and Judith Hanna, *Urban Dynamics in Black Africa* (New York: Aldine, 1981), p. 71.

[27] Leonard Plotnicov, *Strangers to the City: Urban Man in Jos, Nigeria* (Pittsburgh: University of Pittsburgh Press, 1967), pp. 74–75.

[28] Ellen W. Fielding, "Producing and Consuming at White Heat," *Catholicism in Crisis* 3, no. 6 (May 1985): 7.

[29] "Yumpies, YAP's, Yuppies: Who They Are," *US News and World Report* (16 April 1984): 39.

[30] Charles Colson, "A Call to Rescue the Yuppies," *Christianity Today* 29, no. 8 (17 May 1985): 20.

[31] Adrian Hastings, *African Christianity* (New York: Seabury, 1976), p. 84.

[32] Colson, "A Call to Rescue the Yuppies."

[33] Donald McGavran, *Understanding Church Growth,* rev. ed. (Grand Rapids: Wm. B. Eerdmans, 1980), p. 284.

[34] Douglas Butterworth and John Chance, *Latin American Urbanization* (Cambridge: Cambridge University Press, 1981), p. 118.

[35] W. R. Read, V. M. Monterroso, and H. A. Johnson, *Latin American Church Growth* (Grand Rapids: Wm. B. Eerdmans, 1969), p. 229.

[36] Eugene A. Nida, "The Relationship of Social Structure to the Problems of Evangelism in Latin America," in *Readings in Missionary Anthropology,* ed. William A. Smalley (South Pasadena: William Carey Library, 1974), p. 38.

[37] Fred H. Smith, "Growth Through Evangelism," *Urban Mission* 1, no. 1 (September 1983): 24.

[38] Richard Dye, "Church Growth in Acapulco: Planting a Whole Presbytery," *Urban Mission* 3, no. 3 (January 1986): 37–38.

[39] Ibid., p. 38.

[40] "Refugees: A World Overview," in *The Refugees Among Us: Unreached Peoples '83,* ed. Edward Dayton and Samuel Wilson (Monrovia, Calif.: MARC, 1983), p. 177.

[41] Burt N. Singleton, "Finding and Ministering to Refugees," in *The Refugees Among Us: Unreached Peoples '83,* pp. 66–70.

[42] Michael Griffiths, *Changing Asia* (Downers Grove, Ill.: InterVarsity Press, 1977), p. 37.

[43] Orlando Costas, "Evangelizing an Awakening Giant: Hispanics in the U.S.," in *Signs of the Kingdom in the Secular City,* ed. Helen Ujarosy (Chicago: Covenant Press, 1984), p. 56.

[44] Michael Tutterow, "Reaching the Real American," *Mandate: Newsletter of Houston '85,* 1, no. 5 (October 1985): 3.

[45] Peter Wagner, "From 'Melting Pot' to 'Stew Pot': American Social Pluralism and the Church," *Theology, News and Notes* 26, no. 3 (October 1979): 8.

Bibliography

Abrahamson, Mark. *Urban Sociology*. Englewood Cliffs, N.J.: Prentice-Hall, 1980.

Achebe, Chinua. *A Man of the People*. London: Heinemann, 1966.

Adeney, Miriam. *God's Foreign Policy*. Grand Rapids: Wm. B. Eerdmans, 1984.

Arias, Esther, and Mortimer Arias. *The Cry of My People*. New York: Friendship, 1980.

Arias, Mortimer. *Announcing the Reign of God*. Philadelphia: Fortress, 1984.

Bakke, Raymond. "Strategy for Urban Mission." *TSF Bulletin* 8, no. 4 (March–April 1984): 20–21.

―――――. "Urban Evangelization: A Lausanne Strategy Since 1980." *International Bulletin of Missionary Research* 8, no. 4 (October 1984): 149–54.

Baldwin, Leland D. *The American Quest for the City of God*. Macon, Ga.: Mercer University Press, 1981.

Bardo, John W., and John J. Hartman. *Urban Sociology*. Wichita, Kans.: Wichita State University Press, 1982.

Barrett, David B. "Silver and Gold Have I None: Church of the Poor or Church of the Rich?" *International Bulletin of Missionary Research* 7, no. 4 (October 1983): 146–51.

Barth, Karl. *Church Dogmatics*. Vol. 2, pt. 1. Edinburgh: T. and T. Clark, 1955.

Bavinck, J. H. *The Church Between the Temple and the Mosque*. Grand Rapids: Wm. B. Eerdmans, 1982.

Bender, Thomas. *Toward an Urban Vision*. Baltimore: Johns Hopkins University Press, 1978.

Benjamin, Don C. *Deuteronomy and City Life*. Washington: University Press of America, 1983.

Berger, Alan S. *The City: Urban Communities and Their Problems*. Dubuque, Ia.: William C. Brown, 1978.

Best, Ernest E. *Religion and Society in Transition: The Church and Social Change in England, 1560–1850*. New York: Edwin Mellen, 1982.

Blackwell, James E., and Philip S. Hart. *Cities, Suburbs and Blacks: A Study of Concerns, Distrust and Alienation*. Bayside, N.Y.: General Hall, 1982.

Bolton, Robert J. *Treasure Island: Church Growth Among Taiwan's Urban Minnan Chinese.* South Pasadena, Calif.: William Carey Library, 1976.

Bosch, David. *Witness to the World.* London: Marshall, Morgan and Scott, 1980.

Boyer, Paul. *Urban Masses and Moral Order in America, 1820–1920.* Cambridge: Harvard University Press, 1978.

Brandão, Carlos. *Os Deuses do Povo.* São Paulo: Edit. Brasilense, 1980.

Busia, K. A. *Urban Churches in Britain.* London: Lutterworth, 1966.

Butterworth, Douglas, and John K. Chance. *Latin American Urbanization.* Cambridge: Cambridge University Press, 1981.

Cairns, Earle E. *Saints and Sinners.* Chicago: Moody, 1960.

Campolo, Anthony, Jr. *The Power Delusion.* Wheaton, Ill.: Victor, 1983.

Chaney, Charles L. *Church Planting at the End of the Twentieth Century.* Wheaton, Ill.: Tyndale House, 1982.

Christian Witness to Secularized People. Lausanne Occasional Papers, no. 8. Wheaton, Ill.: Lausanne Committee for World Evangelization, 1980.

Chudacoff, Howard P. *The Evolution of American Urban Society.* Englewood Cliffs, N.J.: Prentice-Hall, 1985.

Claerbaut, David. *Urban Ministry.* Grand Rapids: Zondervan, 1983.

"Claiming Turf in Hispanic Chicago." *Eternity* 35, no. 6 (June 1984): 25.

Clowney, Edmund P. "Secularism and the Christian Mission." *Westminster Theological Journal* 21, no. 1 (November 1958): 19–57.

Collins, Thomas, ed. *Cities in a Larger Context.* Athens: University of Georgia Press, 1980.

Colson, Charles. "A Call to Rescue the Yuppies." *Christianity Today* 29, no. 8 (17 May 1985): 17–20.

Conn, Harvie M. *Eternal Word and Changing Worlds: Theology, Anthropology and Mission in Trialogue.* Grand Rapids: Zondervan, 1984.

Cook, William [Guillermo]. "Grass Roots Communities and the 'Protestant Predicament.'" *Occasional Essays* 9, no. 2 (December 1982): 53–86.

──────. "Evangelical Reflections on the Church of the Poor." *Missiology* 11, no. 1 (January 1983): 47–53.

Cornelius, Wayne A., and Robert V. Kemper, eds. *Metropolitan Latin America: The Challenge and the Response.* Beverly Hills: Sage Publications, 1978.

Costas, Orlando. *Christ Outside the Gate.* Maryknoll, N.Y.: Orbis, 1982.

————. "Report on Thailand 80 (Consultation on World Evangelization)." *TSF Bulletin* 4, no. 1 (November 1980): 4–7.

Courtney, Tom. "Mission to the Urban Poor." *Urban Mission* 1, no. 2 (November 1983): 17–24.

Cox, Harvey. "Religion in the Secular City: A Symposium." *Christianity and Crisis* 44, no. 2 (20 February 1984): 35–45.

————. *Religion in the Secular City.* New York: Simon and Schuster, 1984.

————. *The Secular City.* London: SCM Press, 1965.

Cross, Robert D., ed. *The Church and the City, 1865–1910.* Indianapolis: Bobbs-Merrill, 1967.

Dayton, Edward, and Samuel Wilson, eds. *The Future of World Evangelization: Unreached Peoples '84.* Monrovia, Calif.: MARC, 1984.

————. *The Refugees Among Us: Unreached Peoples '83.* Monrovia, Calif.: MARC, 1983.

————. *Unreached Peoples '82.* Elgin, Ill.: David C. Cook, 1982.

Dorchester, Daniel. "The City as a Peril." *National Perils and Opportunities.* New York: Baker and Taylor, 1887. Pages 19–37.

Douglas, Mary. "The Effects of Modernization on Religious Change." *Daedulus* 11, no. 1 (1982): 1–19.

DuBose, Francis. *How Churches Grow in an Urban World.* Nashville: Broadman, 1978.

————. "The Practice of Urban Ministry: Urban Evangelism." *Review and Expositor* 80, no. 4 (Fall 1983): 515–21.

Dudley, Carl S. *Where Have All Our People Gone?* New York: Pilgrim, 1979.

Dye, Richard. "Church Growth in Acapulco: Planting a Whole Presbytery." *Urban Mission* 3, no. 3 (January 1986): 34–39.

Eames, Edwin, and Judith Goode. *Anthropology of the City.* Englewood Cliffs, N.J.: Prentice-Hall, 1977.

Eddy, Elizabeth M., ed. *Urban Anthropology: Research Perspectives and Strategy.* Athens: University of Georgia Press, 1968.

Ellison, Craig, ed. *The Urban Mission.* Grand Rapids: Wm. B. Eerdmans, 1974.

Ellul, Jacques. *The Meaning of the City.* Grand Rapids: Wm. B. Eerdmans, 1970.

Escobar, Samuel, and John Driver. *Christian Mission and Social Justice.* Scottdale, Pa.: Herald, 1978.

Evangelism and Social Responsibility: An Evangelical Commitment. Lausanne Occasional Papers, no. 21. Wheaton, Ill.: Lausanne Committee for World Evangelization, 1982.

"Evangelizing the World-Class Cities." *Together,* no. 2 (January–March 1984): 30–34.

Falk, Peter. *The Growth of the Church in Africa.* Grand Rapids: Zondervan, 1979.

Fielding, Ellen W. "Producing and Consuming at White Heat." *Catholicism in Crisis* 3, no. 6 (May 1985): 7–9.

Forbes, Cheryl. *The Religion of Power.* Grand Rapids: Zondervan, 1983.

Fox, Richard. *Urban Anthropology: Cities in Their Cultural Settings.* Englewood Cliffs, N.J.: Prentice-Hall, 1977.

Frick, Frank S. *The City in Ancient Israel.* Missoula, Mont.: Scholar's Press, 1977.

Funk, Wilfred. *Word Origins.* New York: Bell, 1978.

Gans, Herbert. *Urban Villagers.* Glencoe, Ill.: Free Press, 1962.

Gates, C. W. *Industrialization: Brazil's Catalyst for Church Growth.* South Pasadena: William Carey Library, 1972.

Gilbert, Alan, ed. *Urbanization in Contemporary Latin America.* Chichester, N.Y.: John Wiley, 1982.

Glasner, Peter. *The Sociology of Secularization.* London: Routledge and Kegan Paul, 1977.

Goff, James, and Margaret Goff. *In Every Person Who Hopes . . . .* New York: Friendship, 1980.

Greenway, Roger S. *Calling Our Cities to Christ.* Nutley, N.J.: Presbyterian and Reformed, 1973.

————. "Let These Women Go! Prostitution and the Church." *Urban Mission* 1, no. 4 (March 1984): 17–25.

————. "Reaching the Unreached in the Cites." *Urban Mission* 2, no. 5 (May 1985): 3–5.

————. *An Urban Strategy for Latin America.* Grand Rapids: Baker, 1973.

————, ed. *Discipling the City.* Grand Rapids: Baker, 1979.

————, ed. *Guidelines for Urban Church Planting.* Grand Rapids: Baker, 1976.

Grier, William H., and Price M. Cobbs. *Black Rage.* New York: Bantam, 1969.

Griffiths, Michael. *Changing Asia.* Downers Grove, Ill.: InterVarsity, 1977.

Gugler, Josef, and William G. Flanagan. *Urbanization and Social Change in West Africa*. Cambridge: Cambridge University Press, 1978.

Gutkind, Peter. *Urban Anthropology*. Assen, The Netherlands: Van Gorcum, Ltd., 1974.

Hackler, Tim. "The Big City Has No Corner on Mental Illness." *New York Times Magazine* (19 December 1979): 136, 138.

Hahn, Herbert F. *The Old Testament in Modern Research*. Philadelphia: Fortress, 1966.

Hale, Russell. *The Unchurched: Who They Are and Why They Stay Away*. San Francisco: Harper and Row, 1980.

Hall, Douglas. "Emmanuel Gospel Center, Boston: Contextualized Urban Ministry." *Urban Mission* 1, no. 2 (November 1983): 31–36.

Hanks, Thomas D. *God So Loved the Third World*. Maryknoll, N.Y.: Orbis, 1983.

Hanna, William J., and Judith L. Hanna. *Urban Dynamics in Black Africa*. New York: Aldine, 1981.

Hannerz, Ulf. *Exploring the City*. New York: Columbia University Press, 1980.

Hastings, Adrian. *African Christianity*. New York: Seabury, 1976.

Healey, Joseph G. "Let the Basic Christian Communities Speak." *Missiology* 11, no. 1 (January 1983): 15–30.

Henry, Carl F. H. *A Plea for Evangelical Demonstration*. Grand Rapids: Baker, 1971.

Hinton, Keith. *Growing Churches Singapore Style: Ministry in an Urban Context*. Singapore: OMF Books, 1985.

Holthaus, Lee. "Changing Lives Since 1891: The Union Rescue Mission of Los Angeles." *Urban Mission* 2, no. 2 (November 1984): 5–14.

Hunter, James D. *American Evangelicalism: Conservative Religion and the Quandary of Modernity*. New Brunswick, N.J.: Rutgers University Press, 1983.

"Immigrants and Crime." *United States Immigration Commission,* vol. 36. Washington: Government Printing Office, 1911.

Jacobs, Sylvia M., ed. *Black Americans and the Missionary Movement in Africa*. Westport, Conn.: Greenwood, 1982.

Johnston, Arthur. "Essentials for Urban Ministry." *Alliance Witness* 120, no. 5 (27 February 1985): 9–10.

Kael, Pauline. *When the Lights Go Down*. New York: Rinehart and Winston, 1980.

Kerans, Patrick. *Sinful Social Structures*. New York: Paulist, 1974.

Kingdon, David. "Some Questions About Structural Sin." *Christian Graduate* 33, no. 2 (June 1980): 10–13.

Kuyper, Abraham. *Christianity and the Class Struggle*. Grand Rapids: Piet Hein, 1950.

Ladd, George E. *The Gospel of the Kingdom*. Grand Rapids: Wm. B. Eerdmans, 1954.

Lapidus, Ira M., ed. *Middle Eastern Cities*. Berkeley: University of California Press, 1969.

Lee, Robert, ed. *Cities and Churches: Readings on the Urban Church*. Philadelphia: Westminster, 1962.

Liebow, Elliot. *Tally's Corner*. Boston: Little, Brown, 1967.

Little, Kenneth. *Urbanization as a Social Process: An Essay on Movement and Change in Contemporary Africa*. London: Routledge and Kegan Paul, 1974.

Lloyd, Peter. *Slums of Hope? Shanty Towns of the Third World*. New York: Penguin, 1979.

Loomis, Samuel. *Modern Cities and Their Religious Problems*. New York: Baker and Taylor, 1887.

Lorimer, Frank, and Mark Karp, eds. *Population in Africa*. Boston: Boston University Press, 1960.

Lovelace, Richard F. *Dynamics of Spiritual Life: An Evangelical Theology of Renewal*. Downers Grove, Ill.: InterVarsity, 1979.

Lyon, David. "Secularization: The Fate of Faith in Modern Society." *Themelios* 10, no. 1 (September 1984): 14–22.

—————. *Sociology and the Human Image*. Downers Grove, Ill.: InterVarsity, 1983.

McClory, Robert J. *Racism in America*. Chicago: Fides/Claretian, 1981.

McGavran, Donald A. *Church Growth in Jamaica*. Lucknow: Lucknow, 1962.

—————. *Crucial Issues in Missions Tomorrow*. Chicago: Moody, 1972.

—————. *Understanding Church Growth*, rev. ed. Grand Rapids: Wm. B. Eerdmans, 1980.

—————, ed. *Church Growth and Christian Mission*. New York: Harper and Row, 1965.

McKenna, David, ed. *The Urban Crisis*. Grand Rapids: Zondervan, 1969

McLaughlin, William C. *Modern Revivalism: Charles Grandison Finney to Billy Graham*. New York: Ronald Press, 1955.

"Making the Hotel My Parish." *Bridges* 1, no. 2 (Fall 1984): 4–5.

Marsh, Spencer. *God, Man and Archie Bunker*. New York: Bantam, 1976.

Matheny, Tim. *Reaching the Arabs: A Felt Need Approach.* Pasadena: William Carey Library, 1981.

Maust, John. *Cities of Change: Urban Growth and God's People in Ten Latin American Cities.* Coral Gables, Fla.: Latin America Mission, 1984.

Meeks, Wayne A. *The First Urban Christians.* New Haven: Yale University Press, 1983.

Mennonite Central Committee. *Food and Hunger Notes,* no. 34 (November–December 1985).

Miller, Randall M., and Thomas D. Marzik, eds. *Immigrants and Religion in Urban America.* Philadelphia: Temple University Press, 1977.

Millikan, David. *The Sunburnt Soul: Christianity in Search of an Australian Identity.* Homebush, N.S.W., Australia: Lancer, 1981.

Minear, Paul S. *Images of the Church in the New Testament.* Philadelphia: Westminster, 1960.

Monsma, Timothy. *An Urban Strategy for Africa.* Pasadena: William Carey Library, 1979.

Mouw, Richard J. *Politics and the Biblical Drama.* Grand Rapids: Wm. B. Eerdmans, 1976.

Mumford, Lewis. *The City in History.* New York: Harcourt, Brace, 1961.

Murray, John. *The Claims of Truth.* Vol. 1 of *Collected Writings.* Edinburgh: Banner of Truth Trust, 1976.

_____. *Select Lectures in Systematic Theology.* Vol. 2 of *Collected Writings.* Edinburgh: Banner of Truth Trust, 1977.

Nelson, Amirtharaj. *A New Day in Madras.* South Pasadena: William Carey Library, 1975.

Nelson, Joan. *Access to Power: Politics and the Urban Poor in Developing Nations.* Princeton: Princeton University Press, 1979.

Nisbet, Robert. *History of the Idea of Progress.* New York: Basic Books, 1980.

Okot, P'Bitek. *Song of Lawino.* Nairobi: East African Publ. House, 1966.

Ortiz, Manuel. "A Church in Missiological Tension." *Urban Mission* 2, no. 1 (September 1984): 12–19.

Oswalt, Wendell H. *Understanding Our Culture: An Anthropological View.* New York: Holt, Rinehart and Winston, 1970.

Paget-Wilkes, Michael. *Poverty, Revolution and the Church.* Exeter, Devon: Paternoster, 1981.

Palen, J. John. *The Urban World.* New York: McGraw-Hill, 1981.

Pannenberg, Wolfhart. *Theology and the Kingdom of God.* Philadelphia: Westminster, 1969.

Parvin, Earl. *Missions U.S.A.* Chicago: Moody, 1985.

Pasquariello, Ronald D., Donald W. Shriver, Jr., and Alan Geyer, *Redeeming the City: Theology, Politics and Urban Policy.* New York: Pilgrim, 1982.

Perkins, John. *With Justice for All.* Ventura, Calif.: Regal, 1982.

Perlman, Janice. *The Myth of Marginality.* Berkeley: University of California Press, 1976.

Piet, John. *The Road Ahead: A Theology for the Church in Mission.* Grand Rapids: Wm. B. Eerdmans, 1970.

"The Pioneers." *Latinamerica Press* 16, no. 34 (20 September 1984): 3.

Plotnicov, Leonard. *Strangers to the City: Urban Man in Jos, Nigeria.* Pittsburgh: University of Pittsburgh Press, 1967.

Portes, Alejandro, and John Walton. *Urban Latin America: The Political Condition From Above and Below.* Austin: University of Texas Press, 1976.

Read, William R., Victor M. Monterroso, and Harmon A. Johnson. *Latin American Church Growth.* Grand Rapids: Wm. B. Eerdmans, 1969.

Recker, Robert. "The Redemptive Focus of the Kingdom of God." *Calvin Theological Journal* 14, no. 2 (November 1979): 154–86.

Religion in America: The Gallup Report. Report No. 222. Princeton: Princeton Religion Research Center, 1984.

RES Testimony on Human Rights. Grand Rapids: Reformed Ecumenical Synod, 1983.

Ridderbos, Herman. *Paul: An Outline of His Theology.* Grand Rapids: Wm. B. Eerdmans, 1975.

Roberts, J. Deotis. *Roots of a Black Future: Family and Church.* Philadelphia: Westminster, 1980.

Roberts, Vella-Kottarathil. "The Urban Mission of the Church From an Urban Anthropological Perspective." Unpublished D.Miss. diss., School of World Mission, Fuller Theological Seminary, 1981.

Rose, Larry L., and C. Kirk Hadaway, eds. *The Urban Challenge.* Nashville: Broadman, 1982.

———. *An Urban World: Churches Face the Future.* Nashville: Broadman, 1984.

Roth, Donald R. "Grace Not Race: Southern Negro Church Leaders, Black Identity and Missions to West Africa, 1865-1910." Unpublished Ph.D. diss., University of Texas at Austin, 1975.

Sample, Tex. *Blue Collar Ministry.* Valley Forge: Judson, 1984.

Samuel, Vinay, and Chris Sugden. "Let the Word Become Flesh!" *Third Way* 4, no. 8 (September 1980): 5–8.

Sangster, Verley. *Every Kid*. Denver: Young Life Urban Ministries, 1984.

Schaeffer, Francis A. *Death in the City*. Downers Grove, Ill.: InterVarsity, 1969.

Schmidt, Henry J. "The Urban Ethos: Building Churches in a Pagan Environment." *Mission Focus* 8, no. 2 (June 1980): 25–33.

Schrotenboer, Paul G. *The Meaning of Religion*. Toronto: Association for the Advancement of Christian Scholarship, n.d.

Schwartz, Barry, ed. *The Changing Face of the Suburbs*. Chicago: University of Chicago Press, 1976.

Scott, Waldron. *Bring Forth Justice*. Grand Rapids: Wm. B. Eerdmans, 1980.

"Serving Christ in the City." *The Other Side* 21, no. 5 (July 1985): 8–9.

Shaull, Richard. *Heralds of a New Reformation*. Maryknoll, N.Y.: Orbis, 1984.

Shenk, Wilbert, ed. *Exploring Church Growth*. Grand Rapids: Wm. B. Eerdmans, 1983.

Sheppard, David. *Bias to the Poor*. London: Hodder and Stoughton, Ltd., 1983.

Sherwood, Bill. "Revitalizing Northwest Pasadena." *Bridges* 1, no. 2 (Fall 1984): 10–11.

Shiner, Larry. "The Concept of Secularization in Empirical Research." *Journal for the Scientific Study of Religion* 6 (1967): 207–220.

Sider, Ron. *Rich Christians in an Age of Hunger*. Downers Grove, Ill.: InterVarsity, 1975.

Sine, Tom. *The Mustard Seed Conspiracy*. Waco, Tex.: Word, 1981.

Sjoberg, Gideon. *The Preindustrial City*. New York: Free Press/ Macmillan, 1960.

Smalley, William A., ed. *Readings in Missionary Anthropology*. South Pasadena: William Carey Library, 1974.

Smith, Fred H. "Growth Through Evangelism." *Urban Mission* 1, no. 1 (September 1983): 19–28.

Spates, James L., and John J. Macionis. *The Sociology of Cities*. New York: St. Martin's, 1982.

Steinberg, Stephen. *The Ethnic Myth*. New York: Atheneum, 1981.

Stewart, Edward C. *American Cultural Patterns: A Cross-Cultural Perspective*. LaGrange, Ill.: Intercultural Network, 1972.

Strong, Josiah. *Our Country*. New York: American Home Missionary Society, 1885.

Suttles, Gerald. *The Social Order of the Slum*. Chicago: University of Chicago Press, 1968.

Tate, F. V. "Patterns of Church Growth in Nairobi." Unpublished M.A. thesis, School of World Mission, Fuller Theological Seminary, 1970.

Thailand Report—Christian Witness to Large Cities. Lausanne Occasional Papers, no. 9. Wheaton, Ill.: Lausanne Committee for World Evangelization, 1980.

Thailand Report on the Urban Poor. Lausanne Occasional Papers, no. 22. Wheaton, Ill.: Lausanne Committee for World Evangelization, 1980.

Theissen, Gerd. "Die Starken und Schwaken in Korinth: Soziologische Analyse eines theologischen Streites." *Evangelische Theologie* 35 (1975): 272–89.

Tidball, Derek. *The Social Context of the New Testament*. Grand Rapids: Zondervan, 1984.

Tlapa, Richard J. *The New Apostles: The Mission to the Inner City*. Chicago: Franciscan Herald Press, 1977.

Tonna, Benjamin. *A Gospel for the Cities*. Maryknoll, N.Y.: Orbis, 1982.

Tsai, Kuo-shan. "How to Reach the Industrial Workers in Taiwan." *Chinese Around the World* (June 1985): 4–5.

Tucker, Jerry. "Protestant Ideology and Urban Reform in the United States." Unpublished Ph.D. diss., American University, 1972.

Tuggy, A. L., and R. Oliver. *Seeing the Church in the Philippines*. Manila: OMF Publishers, 1972.

Tutterow, Michael. "Reaching the Real American." *Mandate: Newsletter of Houston '85*, 1, no. 5 (October 1985).

Van Rheenen, Gailyn. *Church Planting in Uganda*. South Pasadena: William Carey Library, 1976.

Vos, Geerhardus. *Biblical Theology*. Grand Rapids: Wm. B. Eerdmans, 1948.

Wagner, C. Peter. "From 'Melting Pot' to 'Stew Pot': American Social Pluralism and the Church." *Theology, News and Notes* 26, no. 3 (October 1979): 4–8.

_____. *Frontiers in Missionary Strategy*. Chicago: Moody, 1971.

Wallis, Jim. *Agenda for Biblical People*. New York: Harper and Row, 1976.

_____. *Revive Us Again: A Sojourner's Story*. Nashville: Abingdon, 1983.

Wasfi, Atif Amin. "Dearborn Arab-Moslem Community: A Study of Acculturation." Unpublished Ph.D. diss., Michigan State University, 1964.

Watson, David. *I Believe in the Church*. Grand Rapids: Wm. B. Eerdmans, 1978.

Weaver, Thomas, and Douglas White, eds. *The Anthropology of Urban Environments*. Washington: Society for Applied Anthropology, 1972.

Webber, George W. *The Congregation in Mission*. Nashville: Abingdon, 1964.

White, Morton, and Lucia White. *The Intellectual Versus the City*. New York: Oxford University Press, 1977.

Williams, Walter L. *Black Americans and the Evangelization of Africa, 1877–1900*. Madison: University of Wisconsin Press, 1982.

Wilson, Bryan. *Religion in Sociological Perspective*. New York: Oxford University Press, 1982.

Winter, Gibson. *The Suburban Captivity of the Church*. Garden City, N.Y.: Doubleday, 1961.

Wolterstorff, Nicholas. *Until Justice and Peace Embrace*. Grand Rapids: Wm. B. Eerdmans, 1983.

"Yumpies, YAP's, Yuppies: Who They Are." *US News and World Report* (16 April 1984): 39.

Ziegenhals, Walter E. *Urban Churches in Transition*. New York: Pilgrim, 1978.

Index of Biblical References

Index of Persons

Lincoln Christian College

Subject Index

236